Modern Critical Views

Chinua Achebe
Henry Adams
Aeschylus
S. Y. Agnon
Edward Albee
Raphael Alberti
Louisa May Alcott
A. R. Ammons
Sherwood Anderson
Aristophanes
Matthew Arnold
Antonin Artaud
John Ashbery
Margaret Atwood
W. H. Auden
Jane Austen
Isaac Babel
Sir Francis Bacon
James Baldwin
Honoré de Balzac
John Barth
Donald Barthelme
Charles Baudelaire
Simone de Beauvoir
Samuel Beckett
Saul Bellow
Thomas Berger
John Berryman
The Bible
Elizabeth Bishop
William Blake
Giovanni Boccaccio
Heinrich Böll
Jorge Luis Borges
Elizabeth Bowen
Bertolt Brecht
The Brontës
Charles Brockden Brown
Sterling Brown
Robert Browning
Martin Buber
John Bunyan
Anthony Burgess
Kenneth Burke
Robert Burns
William Burroughs
George Gordon, Lord
  Byron
Pedro Calderón de la Barca
Italo Calvino
Albert Camus
Canadian Poetry: Modern
  and Contemporary
Canadian Poetry through
  E. J. Pratt
Thomas Carlyle
Alejo Carpentier
Lewis Carroll
Willa Cather
Louis-Ferdinand Céline
Miguel de Cervantes

Geoffrey Chaucer
John Cheever
Anton Chekhov
Kate Chopin
Chrétien de Troyes
Agatha Christie
Samuel Taylor Coleridge
Colette
William Congreve & the
  Restoration Dramatists
Joseph Conrad
Contemporary Poets
James Fenimore Cooper
Pierre Corneille
Julio Cortázar
Hart Crane
Stephen Crane
e. e. cummings
Dante
Robertson Davies
Daniel Defoe
Philip K. Dick
Charles Dickens
James Dickey
Emily Dickinson
Denis Diderot
Isak Dinesen
E. L. Doctorow
John Donne & the
  Seventeenth-Century
  Metaphysical Poets
John Dos Passos
Fyodor Dostoevsky
Frederick Douglass
Theodore Dreiser
John Dryden
W. E. B. Du Bois
Lawrence Durrell
George Eliot
T. S. Eliot
Elizabethan Dramatists
Ralph Ellison
Ralph Waldo Emerson
Euripides
William Faulkner
Henry Fielding
F. Scott Fitzgerald
Gustave Flaubert
E. M. Forster
John Fowles
Sigmund Freud
Robert Frost
Northrop Frye
Carlos Fuentes
William Gaddis
Federico García Lorca
Gabriel García Márquez
André Gide
W. S. Gilbert
Allen Ginsberg
J. W. von Goethe

Nikolai Gogol
William Golding
Oliver Goldsmith
Mary Gordon
Günther Grass
Robert Graves
Graham Greene
Thomas Hardy
Nathaniel Hawthorne
William Hazlitt
H. D.
Seamus Heaney
Lillian Hellman
Ernest Hemingway
Hermann Hesse
Geoffrey Hill
Friedrich Hölderlin
Homer
A. D. Hope
Gerard Manley Hopkins
Horace
A. E. Housman
William Dean Howells
Langston Hughes
Ted Hughes
Victor Hugo
Zora Neale Hurston
Aldous Huxley
Henrik Ibsen
Eugène Ionesco
Washington Irving
Henry James
Dr. Samuel Johnson and
  James Boswell
Ben Jonson
James Joyce
Carl Gustav Jung
Franz Kafka
Yasonari Kawabata
John Keats
Søren Kierkegaard
Rudyard Kipling
Melanie Klein
Heinrich von Kleist
Philip Larkin
D. H. Lawrence
John le Carré
Ursula K. Le Guin
Giacomo Leopardi
Doris Lessing
Sinclair Lewis
Jack London
Robert Lowell
Malcolm Lowry
Carson McCullers
Norman Mailer
Bernard Malamud
Stéphane Mallarmé
Sir Thomas Malory
André Malraux
Thomas Mann

Modern Critical Views

Katherine Mansfield
Christopher Marlowe
Andrew Marvell
Herman Melville
George Meredith
James Merrill
John Stuart Mill
Arthur Miller
Henry Miller
John Milton
Yukio Mishima
Molière
Michel de Montaigne
Eugenio Montale
Marianne Moore
Alberto Moravia
Toni Morrison
Alice Munro
Iris Murdoch
Robert Musil
Vladimir Nabokov
V. S. Naipaul
R. K. Narayan
Pablo Neruda
John Henry Newman
Friedrich Nietzsche
Frank Norris
Joyce Carol Oates
Sean O'Casey
Flannery O'Connor
Christopher Okigbo
Charles Olson
Eugene O'Neill
José Ortega y Gasset
Joe Orton
George Orwell
Ovid
Wilfred Owen
Amos Oz
Cynthia Ozick
Grace Paley
Blaise Pascal
Walter Pater
Octavio Paz
Walker Percy
Petrarch
Pindar
Harold Pinter
Luigi Pirandello
Sylvia Plath
Plato

Plautus
Edgar Allan Poe
Poets of Sensibility & the
   Sublime
Poets of the Nineties
Alexander Pope
Katherine Anne Porter
Ezra Pound
Anthony Powell
Pre-Raphaelite Poets
Marcel Proust
Manuel Puig
Alexander Pushkin
Thomas Pynchon
Francisco de Quevedo
François Rabelais
Jean Racine
Ishmael Reed
Adrienne Rich
Samuel Richardson
Mordecai Richler
Rainer Maria Rilke
Arthur Rimbaud
Edwin Arlington Robinson
Theodore Roethke
Philip Roth
Jean-Jacques Rousseau
John Ruskin
J. D. Salinger
Jean-Paul Sartre
Gershom Scholem
Sir Walter Scott
William Shakespeare
   Histories & Poems
   Comedies & Romances
   Tragedies
George Bernard Shaw
Mary Wollstonecraft
   Shelley
Percy Bysshe Shelley
Sam Shepard
Richard Brinsley Sheridan
Sir Philip Sidney
Isaac Bashevis Singer
Tobias Smollett
Alexander Solzhenitsyn
Sophocles
Wole Soyinka
Edmund Spenser
Gertrude Stein
John Steinbeck

Stendhal
Laurence Sterne
Wallace Stevens
Robert Louis Stevenson
Tom Stoppard
August Strindberg
Jonathan Swift
John Millington Synge
Alfred, Lord Tennyson
William Makepeace Thackeray
Dylan Thomas
Henry David Thoreau
James Thurber and S. J.
   Perelman
J. R. R. Tolkien
Leo Tolstoy
Jean Toomer
Lionel Trilling
Anthony Trollope
Ivan Turgenev
Mark Twain
Miguel de Unamuno
John Updike
Paul Valéry
Cesar Vallejo
Lope de Vega
Gore Vidal
Virgil
Voltaire
Kurt Vonnegut
Derek Walcott
Alice Walker
Robert Penn Warren
Evelyn Waugh
H. G. Wells
Eudora Welty
Nathanael West
Edith Wharton
Patrick White
Walt Whitman
Oscar Wilde
Tennessee Williams
William Carlos Williams
Thomas Wolfe
Virginia Woolf
William Wordsworth
Jay Wright
Richard Wright
William Butler Yeats
A. B. Yehoshua
Emile Zola

Modern Critical Views

TENNESSEE WILLIAMS

Edited and with an introduction by

Harold Bloom
Sterling Professor of the Humanities
Yale University

CHELSEA HOUSE PUBLISHERS
New York ◇ Philadelphia

© 1987 by Chelsea House Publishers, a division
of Main Line Book Co.

Introduction © 1987 by Harold Bloom

Printed and bound in the United States of America

10   9   8

∞ The paper used in this publication meets the minimum
requirements of the American National Standard for
Permanence of Paper for Printed Library Materials,
Z39.48-1984.

Library of Congress Cataloging-in-Publication Data
Tennessee Williams.
      (Modern critical views)
      Bibliography: p.
      Includes index.
      Summary: A collection of critical essays on Williams and
his works arranged in chronological order of publication.
      1. Williams, Tennessee, 1911–   —Criticism and
interpretation.   [1. Williams, Tennessee, 1911–
—Criticism and interpretation.   2. American literature.
—History and criticism]   I.   Bloom, Harold.   II. Series.
PS3545.I5365Z843   1987   812'.54   86-23236
ISBN 0-87754-636-3

Contents

Editor's Note

This book gathers together what seems to me the best criticism available upon the plays of Tennessee Williams, reprinted here in the chronological order in which these essays and reviews first appeared. I am grateful to Henry Finder and Edward Jefferson for their aid in editing this volume.

My introduction begins with a consideration of Williams as a dramatic lyricist in the mode of Hart Crane, rather than as a lyrical dramatist in the mode of Chekhov. My general argument is then pursued in exegeses of *The Glass Menagerie* and *A Streetcar Named Desire*.

Alvin B. Kernan, eminent scholar-critic of the drama in its full historical development, begins the chronological sequence with a brief but pungent contrast between the "realistic" (Stanley) and "romantic" (Blanche) visions in *Streetcar*. With Joseph Riddel's reading of the play, we are given a Nietzschean critique of Williams's failure to curb his realism in the interests of a Dionysian perspective.

In a Jungian exegesis that centers upon *Cat on a Hot Tin Roof*, Esther Merle Jackson emphasizes Williams's failure to achieve convincing images of aesthetic transcendence of spiritual dilemmas. Comparing *Orpheus Descending* with its earlier version as *Battle of Angels*, Leonard Quirino attempts to uncover Williams's obsessive quest for a metaphysical horror buried in the heart of our existence.

Ruby Cohn returns us to the early plays, exploring their origins in previous works and finding in them an authentic contribution to American stage dialogue. In some illuminating remarks on the middle plays, culminating with *The Milk Train Doesn't Stop Here Anymore*, Robert B. Heilman explores the trope of salvation in Williams. Thomas L. King discusses Tom's soliloquies in *The Glass Menagerie* and concludes that only Laurette Taylor's luminous performance as Amanda can account for the critical neglect of Tom—*the* central character of the play. *Camino Real*, one of the most problematic plays of our time, is seen by James Coakley as "a dark message in the garish colors of a circus sideshow." A desperate moralism, awash in the realms of the self, is analyzed by Arthur Ganz in an overview of Williams's achievement.

Another perspective, quite different from that offered in my introduction, is opened upon the influence relation between Hart Crane and Williams by Gilbert Debusscher. In the final essay of this volume, the British critic C. W. E. Bigsby investigates the later Williams, and sums up the dramatist's career by citing the younger playwright David Mamet, who identified Williams's true subject as the American malaise of not knowing how to show our love.

Introduction

I

It is a sad and inexplicable truth that the United States, a dramatic nation, continues to have so limited a literary achievement in the drama. American literature, from Emerson to the present moment, is a distinguished tradition. The poetry of Whitman, Dickinson, Frost, Stevens, Eliot, W. C. Williams, Hart Crane, R. P. Warren, Elizabeth Bishop down through the generation of my own contemporaries—John Ashbery, James Merrill, A. R. Ammons and others—has an unquestionable eminence, and takes a vital place in Western literature. Prose fiction from Hawthorne and Melville on through Mark Twain and Henry James to Cather and Dreiser, Faulkner, Hemingway, Fitzgerald, Nathanael West, and Pynchon, has almost a parallel importance. The line of essayists and critics from Emerson and Thoreau to Kenneth Burke and beyond constitutes another crucial strand of our national letters. But where is the American drama in comparison to all this, and in relation to the long cavalcade of Western drama from Aeschylus to Beckett?

The American theater, by the common estimate of its most eminent critics, touches an initial strength with Eugene O'Neill, and then proceeds to the more varied excellences of Thornton Wilder, Tennessee Williams, Arthur Miller, Edward Albee, and Sam Shepard. That sequence is clearly problematical, and becomes even more worrisome when we move from playwrights to plays. Which are our dramatic works that matter most? *A Long Day's Journey Into Night*, certainly; perhaps *The Iceman Cometh*; evidently *A Streetcar Named Desire* and *Death of a Salesman*; perhaps again *The Skin of Our Teeth* and *The Zoo Story*—it is not God's plenty. And I will venture the speculation that our drama palpably is not yet literary enough. By this I do not just mean that O'Neill writes very badly, or Miller very baldly; they do, but so did Dreiser, and *Sister Carrie* and *An American Tragedy* prevail nevertheless. Nor do I wish to be an American Matthew Arnold (whom I loathe above all other critics) and proclaim that our dramatists simply have

1

not known enough. They know more than enough, and that is part of the trouble.

Literary tradition, as I have come to understand it, masks the agon between past and present as a benign relationship, whether personal or societal. The actual transferences between the force of the literary past and the potential of writing in the present tend to be darker, even if they do not always or altogether follow the defensive patterns of what Sigmund Freud called "family romances." Whether or not an ambivalence, however repressed, towards the past's force is felt by the new writer and is manifested in his work seems to depend entirely upon the ambition and power of the oncoming artist. If he aspires after strength, and can attain it, then he must struggle with both a positive and a negative transference, false connections because necessarily imagined ones, between a composite precursor and himself. His principal resource in that agon will be his own native gift for interpretation, or as I am inclined to call it, strong misreading. Revising his precursor, he will create himself, make himself into a kind of changeling, and so he will become, in an illusory but highly pragmatic way, his own father.

The most literary of our major dramatists, and clearly I mean "literary" in a precisely descriptive sense, neither pejorative nor eulogistic, was Tennessee Williams. Wilder, with his intimate connections to *Finnegans Wake* and Gertrude Stein, might seem to dispute this placement, and Wilder was certainly more literate than Williams. But Wilder had a benign relation to his crucial precursor, Joyce, and did not aspire after a destructive strength. Williams did, and suffered the fate he prophesied and desired; the strength destroyed his later work, and his later life, and thus joined itself to the American tradition of self-destructive genius. Williams truly had one precursor only: Hart Crane, the greatest of our lyrical poets, after Whitman and Dickinson, and the most self-destructive figure in our national literature, surpassing all others in this, as in so many regards.

Williams asserted he had other precursors also: D. H. Lawrence, and Chekhov in the drama. These were outward influences, and benefited Williams well enough, but they were essentially formal, and so not the personal and societal family romance of authentic poetic influence. Hart Crane made Williams into more of a dramatic lyrist, though writing in prose, than the lyrical dramatist that Williams is supposed to have been. Though this influence—perhaps more nearly an identification—helped form *The Glass Menagerie* and (less overtly) *A Streetcar Named Desire*, and in a lesser mode *Summer and Smoke* and *Suddenly Last Summer*, it also led to such disasters of misplaced lyricism as the dreadful *Camino Real* and the dreary *The Night of the Iguana*.

(*Cat on a Hot Tin Roof,* one of Williams's best plays, does not seem to me to show any influence of Crane.) Williams's long aesthetic decline covered thirty years, from 1953 to 1983, and reflected the sorrows of a seer who, by his early forties, had outlived his own vision. Hart Crane, self-slain at thirty-two, had set for Williams a High Romantic paradigm that helped cause Williams, his heart as dry as summer dust, to burn to the socket.

II

In Hart Crane's last great Pindaric ode, "The Broken Tower," the poet cries aloud, in a lament that is also a high celebration, the destruction of his battered self by his overwhelming creative gift:

> The bells, I say, the bells break down their tower;
> And swing I know not where. Their tongues engrave
> Membrane through marrow, my long-scattered score
> Of broken intervals . . . And I, their sexton slave!

This Shelleyan and Whitmanian catastrophe creation, or death by inspiration, was cited once by Williams as an omen of Crane's self-immolation. "By the bells breaking down their tower," in Williams's interpretation, Crane meant "the romantic and lyric intensity of his vocation." Gilbert Debusscher has traced the intensity of Crane's effect upon Williams's Romantic and lyric vocation, with particular reference to Tom Wingfield's emergent vocation in *The Glass Menagerie.* More than forty years after its first publication, the play provides an absorbing yet partly disappointing experience of rereading.

A professed "memory play," *The Glass Menagerie* seems to derive its continued if wavering force from its partly repressed representation of the quasi-incestuous and doomed love between Tom Wingfield and his crippled, "exquisitely fragile," ultimately schizophrenic sister Laura. Incest, subtly termed the most poetical of circumstances by Shelley, is the dynamic of the erotic drive throughout Williams's more vital writings. Powerfully displaced, it is the secret dynamic of what is surely Williams's masterwork, *A Streetcar Named Desire.*

The Glass Menagerie scarcely bothers at such a displacement, and the transparency of the incest motif is at once the play's lyrical strength and, alas, its dramatic weakness. Consider the moment when Williams chooses to end the play, which times Tom's closing speech with Laura's gesture of blowing out the candles:

> TOM: I didn't go to the moon, I went much further—for time is
> the longest distance between two places. Not long after

that I was fired for writing a poem on the lid of a shoe-
box. I left St. Louis. I descended the steps of this fire
escape for a last time and followed, from then on, in my
father's footsteps, attempting to find in motion what was
lost in space. I traveled around a great deal. The cities
swept about me like dead leaves, leaves that were brightly
colored but torn away from the branches. I would have
stopped, but I was pursued by something. It always came
upon me unawares, taking me altogether by surprise.
Perhaps it was a familiar bit of music. Perhaps it was only
a piece of transparent glass. Perhaps I am walking along a
street at night, in some strange city, before I have found
companions. I pass the lighted window of a shop where
perfume is sold. The window is filled with pieces of
colored glass, tiny transparent bottles in delicate colors,
like bits of a shattered rainbow. Then all at once my sister
touches my shoulder. I turn around and look into her
eyes. Oh, Laura, Laura, I tried to leave you behind me,
but I am more faithful than I intended to be! I reach for a
cigarette, I cross the street, I run into the movies or a bar,
I buy a drink, I speak to the nearest stranger—anything
that can blow your candles out!

[*Laura bends over the candles.*]

For nowadays the world is lit by lightning! Blow out your
candles, Laura—and so goodbye. . . .

[*She blows the candles out.*]

The many parallels between the lives and careers of Williams and Crane
stand behind this poignant passage, though it is fascinating that the actual
allusions and echoes here are to Shelley's poetry, but then Shelley increasingly appears to be Crane's heroic archetype, and one remembers Robert
Lowell's poem where Crane speaks and identifies himself as the Shelley of
his age. The cities of aesthetic exile sweep about Wingfield/Williams like
the dead, brightly colored leaves of the "Ode to the West Wind," dead leaves
that are at once the words of the poet and lost human souls, like the beloved
sister Laura.

What pursues Tom is what pursues the Shelleyan Poet of *Alastor*, an
avenging daimon or shadow of rejected, sisterly eros that manifests itself in
a further Shelleyan metaphor, the shattered, colored transparencies of Shel-

ley's dome of many-colored glass in *Adonais*, the sublime, lyrical elegy for Keats. That dome, Shelley says, is a similitude for life, and its many colors stain the white radiance of Eternity until death tramples the dome into fragments. Williams beautifully revises Shelley's magnificent trope. For Williams, life itself, through memory as its agent, shatters itself and scatters the colored transparencies of the rainbow, which ought to be, but is not, a covenant of hope.

As lyrical prose, this closing speech has its glory, but whether the dramatic effect is legitimate seems questionable. The key sentence, dramatically, is: "Oh, Laura, Laura, I tried to leave you behind me, but I am more faithful than I intended to be!" In his descriptive list of the characters, Williams says of his surrogate, Wingfield: "His nature is not remorseless, but to escape from a trap he has to act without pity." What would pity have been? And in what sense is Wingfield more faithful, after all, than he attempted to be?

Williams chooses to end the play as though its dramatic center had been Laura, but every reader and every playgoer knows that every dramatic element in the play emanates out from the mother, Amanda. Dream and its repressions, guilt and desire, have remarkably little to do with the representation of Amanda in the play, and everything to do with her children. The split between dramatist and lyrist in Williams is manifested in the play as a generative divide. Williams's true subject, like Crane's, is the absolute identity between his artistic vocation and his homosexuality. What is lacking in *The Glass Menagerie* is that Williams could not have said of Amanda, what, Flaubert-like, he did say of the heroine of *Streetcar*: "I am Blanche DuBois." There, and there only, Williams could fuse Chekhov and Hart Crane into one.

III

The epigraph to *A Streetcar Named Desire* is a quatrain from Hart Crane's "The Broken Tower," the poet's elegy for his gift, his vocation, his life, and so Crane's precise equivalent of Shelley's *Triumph of Life*, Keats's *Fall of Hyperion*, and Whitman's "When Lilacs Last in the Dooryard Bloom'd." Tennessee Williams, in his long thirty years of decline after composing *A Streetcar Named Desire*, had no highly designed, powerfully executed elegy for his own poetic self. Unlike Crane, his American Romantic precursor and aesthetic paradigm, Williams had to live out the slow degradation of the waning of his potential, and so endured the triumph of life over his imagination.

Streetcar sustains a first rereading, after thirty years away from it, more strongly than I had expected. It is, inevitably, more remarkable on the stage than in the study, but the fusion of Williams's lyrical and dramatic talents in it has prevailed over time, at least so far. The play's flaws, in performance, ensue from its implicit tendency to sensationalize its characters, Blanche DuBois in particular. Directors and actresses have made such sensationalizing altogether explicit, with the sad result prophesied by Kenneth Tynan twenty-five years ago. The playgoer forgets that Blanche's only strengths are "nostalgia and hope," that she is "the desperate exceptional woman," and that her fall is a parable, rather than an isolated squalor:

> When, finally, she is removed to the mental home, we should feel that a part of civilization is going with her. Where ancient drama teaches us to reach nobility by contemplation of what is noble, modern American drama conjures us to contemplate what might have been noble, but is now humiliated, ignoble in the sight of all but the compassionate.

Tynan, though accurate enough, still might have modified the image of Blanche taking a part of civilization away with her into madness. Though Blanche yearns for the values of the aesthetic, she scarcely embodies them, being in this failure a masochistic self-parody on the part of Williams himself. His *Memoirs* portray Williams incessantly in the role of Blanche, studying the nostalgias, and inching along the wavering line between hope and paranoia. Williams, rather than Blanche, sustains Tynan's analysis of the lost nobility, now humiliated, that American drama conjures us to contemplate.

The fall of Blanche is a parable, not of American civilization's lost nobility, but of the failure of the American literary imagination to rise above its recent myths of recurrent defeat. Emerson admonished us, his descendants, to go beyond the Great Defeat of the Crucifixion and to demand Victory instead, a victory of the senses as well as of the soul. Walt Whitman, taking up Emerson's challenge directly, set the heroic pattern so desperately emulated by Hart Crane, and which is then repeated in a coarser tone in Williams's life and work.

It must seem curious, at first, to regard Blanche DuBois as a failed Whitmanian, but essentially that is her aesthetic identity. Confronted by the revelation of her young husband's preference for an older man over herself, Blanche falls downwards and outwards into nymphomania, phantasmagoric hopes, pseudo-imaginative collages of memory and desire. Her Orphic, psychic rending by the amiably brutal Stanley Kowalski, a rough but effective version of D. H. Lawrence's vitalistic vision of male force, is pathetic rather than tragic, not because Stanley necessarily is mindless, but because she unnecessarily has made herself mindless, by failing the pragmatic test of experience.

Williams's most effective blend of lyrical vision and dramatic irony in the play comes in the agony of Blanche's cry against Stanley to Stella, his wife and her sister:

> He acts like an animal, has an animal's habits! Eats like one, moves like one, talks like one! There's even something—sub-human—something not quite to the stage of humanity yet! Yes, something—ape-like about him, like one of those pictures I've seen in—anthropological studies! Thousands and thousands of years have passed him right by, and there he is—Stanley Ko-walski—survivor of the stone age! Bearing the raw meat home from the kill in the jungle! And you—*you* here—*waiting* for him! Maybe he'll strike you or maybe grunt and kiss you! That is, if kisses have been discovered yet! Night falls and the other apes gather! There in the front of the cave, all grunting like him, and swilling and gnawing and hulking! His poker night!—you call it—this party of apes! Somebody growls—some creature snatches at something—the fight is on! *God!* Maybe we are a long way from being made in God's image, but Stella—my sister—there has been *some* progress since then! Such things as art—as poetry and music—such kinds of new light have come into the world since then! In some kinds of people some tenderer feelings have had some little beginning! That we have got to make *grow!* And *cling* to, and hold as our flag! In this dark march toward whatever it is we're approaching. . . . *Don't—don't hang back with the brutes!*

The lyricism here takes its strength from the ambivalence of what at once attracts and dismays both Blanche and Williams. Dramatic irony, ter-rible in its antithetical pathos, results here from Blanche's involuntary self-condemnation, since she herself has hung back with the brutes while merely blinking at the new light of the aesthetic. Stanley, being what he is, is clearly less to blame than Blanche, who was capable of more but failed in will.

Williams, in his *Memoirs*, haunted as always by Hart Crane, refers to his precursor as "a tremendous and yet fragile artist," and then associates both himself and Blanche with the fate of Crane, a suicide by drowning in the Caribbean:

I am as much of an hysteric as . . . Blanche; a codicil to my will
provides for the disposition of my body in this way. "Sewn up
in a clean white sack and dropped over board, twelve hours north
of Havana, so that my bones may rest not too far from those of
Hart Crane . . ."

At the conclusion of *Memoirs*, Williams again associated Crane both with
his own vocation and his own limitations, following Crane even in an identification with the young Rimbaud:

A poet such as the young Rimbaud is the only writer of whom
I can think, at this moment, who could escape from words into
the sensations of being, through his youth, turbulent with rev-
olution, permitted articulation by nights of absinthe. And of
course there is Hart Crane. Both of these poets touched fire that
burned them alive. And perhaps it is only through self-immolation of such a nature that we living beings can offer to you the
entire truth of ourselves within the reasonable boundaries of a
book.

It is the limitation of *Memoirs*, and in some sense even of *A Streetcar
Named Desire*, that we cannot accept either Williams or poor Blanche as a
Rimbaud or a Hart Crane. Blanche cannot be said to have touched fire that
burned her alive. Yet Williams earns the relevance of the play's great epigraph
to Blanche's terrible fate:

> And so it was I entered the broken world
> To trace the visionary company of love, its voice
> An instant in the wind (I know not whither hurled)
> But not for long to hold each desperate choice.

ALVIN B. KERNAN

Truth and Dramatic Mode
in A Streetcar Named Desire

Both Chekhov and Pirandello created plays written in a mixture of modes which bring the individual and his suffering into relief, but they do so only by ignoring any power which transcends man and forces him to certain decisions. Some qualification of this statement is required to adjust it to Chekhov, . . . but by and large both the dramatists discussed show humanity in a purely human setting. Man can understand himself by understanding others. Tennessee Williams recognizes this as a possibility, but he cannot as Pirandello and Chekhov do, simply deny the validity of the realistic perspective. His plays are unresolved battles between Pirandello's stage-manager and the Characters, and his heroes are usually, though not always, mixtures of Dorn and Trepleff. In each of his plays, Williams poises the human need for belief in human value and dignity against a brutal, naturalistic reality; similarly, symbolism is poised against realism. But where the earlier playwrights were able to concentrate on human values, Williams has been unable to do so because of his conviction that there is a "real" world outside and inside each of us which is actively hostile to any belief in the goodness of man and the validity of moral values. His realism gives expression to this aspect of the world, and *A Streetcar Named Desire* is his clearest treatment of the human dilemma which entails the dramatic dilemma. We are presented in *Streetcar* with two polar ways of looking at experience: the realistic view of Stanley Kowalski and the "non-realistic" view of his sister-in-law, Blanche Du Bois. Williams brings the two views into conflict immediately.

From *Modern Drama* 1, no. 2 (September 1958). © 1958 by the University of Toronto, Graduate Centre for the Study of Drama.

When Blanche first arrives in the "Elysian Fields" she is terrified by its shabbiness, animality, and dirt, and, pointing vaguely out the window, says, "Out there I suppose is the ghoul-haunted woodland of Weir!" Her sister, Stella, replies, "No, honey, those are the L & N tracks." This is the basic problem which has kept the modern theater boiling: Is the modern world best described as a "ghoul-haunted woodland" or a neutrally denominated something like "The L & N tracks?" The question is kept open in *Streetcar* in a number of ways. Stanley, suspicious about the amount of clothes and jewelry that Blanche has, decides that she has cheated Stella, and therefore himself, of her inheritance of the old plantation. He, however, mistakes rhinestones for diamonds, junk jewelry for genuine, imitation furs for white fox, and a mortgage-ridden, twenty-acre, decayed plantation for a cotton kingdom. The mistake is the mistake of the realist who trusts to literal appearances, to his senses alone.

In the course of the play Williams manages to identify this realism with the harsh light of the naked electric bulb which Blanche covers with a Japanese lantern. It reveals pitilessly every line in Blanche's face, every tawdry aspect of the set. And in just this way Stanley's pitiless and probing realism manages to reveal every line in Blanche's soul by cutting through all the soft illusions with which she has covered herself. But it is important to note that it is an artificial light, not a natural one, which reveals Blanche as old and cheap. She is so only when judged by a way of looking at things which insists that the senses are the only true measure of things, and only that is real which is a "thing."

But while the play makes clear the limitations of realism as an approach to experience, it makes it equally clear that this view must be accepted, however much we may dislike it; and Williams here and in his other plays dislikes it a great deal. The "realistic" point of view has the advantage of being workable. Blanche's romantic way of looking at things, sensitive as it may be, has a fatal weakness: it exists only by ignoring certain portions of reality. This is shown in a number of ways in *Streetcar*, principally in Blanche's refusal to face up to certain acts of her past and the present reality of her own sexual drives which she covers over with such words as "flirting." The movement of the play is towards a stripping away of these pretensions and culminates in the scene where Stanley rapes Blanche. As Stanley destroys each of Blanche's pretensions, pointing out that she didn't "pull any wool over this boy's eyes," Blanche tries desperately to telephone for help, but doesn't know the address. She turns to the window, still looking for help, and looks at the *facts:* "A prostitute has rolled a drunkard. He pursues her along the walk, overtakes her and there is a struggle. A policeman's whistle breaks it up . . . Some moments later the Negro Woman appears around the corner with a sequined bag which the prostitute had dropped on the walk. She is rooting excitedly through it." Here is reality, "raw and lurid," the animal struggle for existence which has replaced the bourgeois drawing room in the modern theater. Yet Blanche has always known these facts. Her husband turned out to be a pervert, then committed suicide. Belle Reve was mortgaged away to provide for the "epic fornications" of her ancestors, and death in its most terrible shapes made its home in her house for many years. When reproached by Mitch for deception she replies, simply, "I didn't lie in my heart." Just as she had turned from the death in Belle Reve to the "life" of casual *amours*, so she had turned away from the misery of "reality" to her romantic evasions. But Stanley hates her, has to prove his dominance, and after analyzing her in his own "realistic" terms, rapes her. Reality has forced itself on her, and she has no way left to travel except madness and death. She cannot live with what Williams and most men of our time unhappily regard as reality.

But it remains for Stella to make a choice. She stands between these two, for they are the pure products of their respective views while Stella, like most humans, participates in both, born kin to the "romantic" and married to the "realistic." Her moral sense is still active, for she points out to Eunice that "I couldn't believe [Blanche's] story and go on living with Stanley." Eunice's answer contains the dreadful truth of our times, "Don't ever believe it. Life has got to go on. No matter what happens, you've got to keep on going." Man, then, says the play, has a moral sense and an aesthetic sense which looks on the world and names it correctly "The ghoul-haunted woodland of Weir," but such knowledge is useless though not untrue. Useless because you can only live in that Woodland if you rob it of all its terrors by giving it the neutral and spiritually empty denomination of "The L & N tracks." This is the pragmatic test, and behind it lies the only "truth" that Williams will maintain, "you've got to keep on going."

For Williams, as for Pirandello, the "truth" of Nature is undefinable. He only knows that the face it turns toward us is brutal and savage, the "real camino," not the "Camino Real." But rather than trying to penetrate it he falls back on showing that "realism" is simply a man-made mode of coming to terms with a world it could not otherwise face. Yet Williams's violent fluctuations between expressionism and a Zolaesque realism, his delight in rich symbolism even in the midst of his most realistic plays, suggest a sensitive awareness of absolute moral values and of a Nature which transcends the misery of the "Elysian Fields."

JOSEPH N. RIDDEL

A Streetcar Named Desire—
Nietzsche Descending

To see *A Streetcar Named Desire* as a realistic slice-of-life is to mistake its ambitious theme; to find it social protest is to misread the surface, for just as in *The Glass Menagerie*, Williams gets in his social licks while groping for a more universal statement. It is not, however, in its subthemes that *Streetcar* fails but in its overabundant intellectualism, its aspiration to say something about man and his civilization, its eclectic use and often contradictory exploitation of ideas. Williams has been called neo-Lawrencean, placing him in that assemblage of revived romantics and primitives in revolt against a sodden, effeminate age, but he is a Nietzschean as well, if in a very imperfect and perhaps over-impetuous way.

In *Streetcar*, as in several other plays, Williams borrows from Nietzsche in great chunks, often undigested, using his sources with that liberal freedom that has become characteristic of the American artist in search of a theme. Readers of *Streetcar* are soon aware of the problems this creates, for they are faced at the beginning by a welter of symbols—both linguistic and theatrical—that force upon the realistic surface a conscious, almost allegorical pattern. Williams has, at various times, had less success with the integration of his excessive symbolism and his theme, as in the satyr-like spiritualism of *The Rose Tattoo* or the panic-homosexual-psychoanalytic motif of *Suddenly Last Summer*. But even in *Streetcar* one must begin with a contradiction between his intellectual design and the militant primitivism of the theme;

From *Modern Drama* 5, no. 4 (February 1963). © 1963 by the University of Toronto, Graduate Centre for the Study of Drama.

or to use a philosophical gloss, one must begin with Nietzsche's Apollonian-Dionysian conflict, in an almost literal sense.

Williams has offered what he considers a serious rationale for his kind of drama in "The Timeless World of a Play," with which he prefaced an edition of *The Rose Tattoo*. The argument is dubious but revealing. As if he had misinterpreted Eliot's remark, that art expresses a primitive truth which uses the phenomena of civilization because that is all it has to use, Williams makes a plea for the drama as a non-temporal stage whose characters are removed from and purified of their distracting social contexts. The play, he insists, arrests time, snatching the "eternal out of the desperately fleeting," penetrating beyond the social façade to the innate man beneath. Anyone familiar with the devices of *The Glass Menagerie* will recognize that he is to take a cue from the opening and closing sequences and filter out the tawdriness of the middle, the mundane stuff that blights the purity of the characters' hearts and actions. Life, it implies, is maligned by the conditions of living. There is more than social protest here, and there is certainly no area for the tragic.

This strangely persistent romantic notion that the idea of man is some pre-rational, mystical, universal oneness which civilization with its artificial forms travesties is indifferent to the artist's strategic assumption that between man and his conditions there is indeed a plausible and symbolic connection. What Kenneth Burke has termed the strategy of scene-act ratio is certainly fundamental to a fully realized stage, from the mythic to the realistic—as Francis Fergusson's important study, *The Idea of a Theater*, proves. (One can make this observation, I think, without being callous about social inequity or injustice, without saying that each man deserves his environment.) Williams himself depends extensively on the symbolic ratio of character to scene, yet he seems to ask for two contradictory things: that we endure his realistic surface—and indeed be entertained and informed by it—and that we respond more truly by extirpating the temporal and spiritually involving ourselves in the purified world beneath. In effect, the symbolic scene should add meaningful dimensions to the play, yet not be a temporal setting at all. Furthermore, he is insisting that in the drama individuation of character is only a convenience and that character finally resolves into the archetypes of a morality play—or better, a pre-morality dance of life. This is something else again than saying that a character must be universal; it claims that he is pure essence. In sum, it is a rather narrow variation on the prevailing critical thesis of drama as ritual, only Williams, instead of making the valid observation that characters constitute parts of a whole in the play, steps outside drama to postulate a spiritual, primordial idea of man which the play evokes.

In *The Birth of Tragedy*, Nietzsche describes the difference between the chorus and the virgins bearing laurel branches, in his characteristic Greek play, as a symbolic antithesis of the Dionysian and the Apollonian: the one characterized by a oneness of passion and metaphysical character, the other by restraint, order, and by individuation of character. His metaphysical tension between the Dionysian and the Apollonian natures is, in the simplest terms, his definition of tragedy; but as Walter Kaufmann has convincingly shown, to accentuate the Dionysian at the expense of its antithesis, as is popularly done, is to misread Nietzsche's famous metaphor. Indeed, says Kaufmann, Nietzsche is the Apollonian at heart, who has come to recognize the effeteness of civilization that exhausts or extirpates its vital creative energies (its Dionysian self) in empty forms, that sacrifices vitality for order. The Dionysian spirit, then, he finds necessary but potentially chaotic, unless channeled and put to creative use by the Apollonian. In Greek drama at its height Nietzsche discovered just the proper tension—so necessary to his conception of man's tragic dignity—before the intrusion of Socratic reason, admirable as it was, led to a forced exclusion of the Dionysian vitality, and subsequently, in secular epigenism and Christianity, to an ethical world view that sought to suppress all disordered passions. The point of all this is that Nietzsche, the supposed progenitor of post-ethical romanticism, is an antagonist of romanticism, which he repudiated in a later preface to *The Birth of Tragedy* as a kind of unrestrained, chaotic investment in emotion for emotion's sake. In his later work, Kaufmann shows, Nietzsche reconstructed Dionysus in the character of an ideal divinity (a combination of Dionysus-Apollo), so that the repudiated Dionysus and the one with whom Nietzsche at last identified himself are two different gods. In sum, Nietzsche's conception was dialectical, Dionysus needing Apollo like the id an ego, or vitality form; and ultimately the two blend in an ideal of tragic beauty. It is the influence of Jung, with his radically romantic world of archetypes, that has done so much to motivate our artist's return to the primitive, but the misplaced emphasis on Nietzsche's Dionysus is no less important.

Willfully or not, Williams seems to commit the error of popular misinterpretation, not in the sense that he writes a drama to the Nietzschean tune but that he exploits Nietzsche's metaphor to elucidate and justify his own vaguely formed vision of man. At times his play gains intensity of realization from his obsession with the conflict between creative impulse and civilized decorum; on other occasions it suffers from a divisiveness caused by its lack of tension, its undialectical character, its deliberately one-sided argument. This very lack of tension—thematic not dramatic—precludes tragedy and leaves us in a very startling way with a thesis play of sorts and a series of violent if symbolic actions.

The setting of *Streetcar* is a combination of raw realism and deliberate fantasy, a world very much of our society yet timeless and innocent, without ethical dimensions. Williams's evocation of a mythical Elysia suggests a world of the guiltless, of spring and sunlight (though his is shaded, a night world), a pre-Christian paradise where life and passion are one and good. The "Elysian Fields" is New Orleans in several senses: the Elysia where life is pursued on a primitive level beyond or before good and evil. This, I think, must be insisted upon, for the play is a deliberate outrage against conventional morality, a kind of immoralist's protest in the manner if not the style of Gide. The impressionistic scene, lyrical and with an aura of vitality that "attenuates the atmosphere of decay," is a Dionysian world of oneness, where there is an "easy mingling of races" and the pagan chromatics of a "blue piano" provide rhythms for a Bacchic revel.

One does not have to force his interpretation. The humorous vulgarity of the opening section is self-consciously symbolic, abrupt on the level of realism but carefully designed to signify the play's two worlds. Stanley's appearance in his masculine vigor, carrying a "red stained package from the butcher's," competes with the mythical aura of the scene. The implied virility of his gesture in tossing the package to Stella, her suggestive response, and the carefree vigor of their unconcern with time defines succinctly a kind of world that is immediate yet infused with an intensity beyond the real. The scene then pans down on Blanche in her demure and fragile dress, garishly overrefined, overwhelmed by life, out of place in Elysium. She has arrived, we learn, by way of a Freudian streetcar named "Desire," transferring to one called "Cemeteries." The psychoanalytic devices are obvious: Stanley's gesture is vital—prurient yet pure; Blanche on her figurative streetcars has been a pawn of the phallus of desire. If she is a cliché of southern literature, she is likewise the incarnate deathwish of civilization. Williams takes his epigraph from Hart Crane's "The Broken Tower," and perhaps also his streetcar from Crane's "For the Marriage of Faustus and Helen," though the poet's work soon jumps its Freudian tracks to become his Faustian artist's symbolic conveyance to a Helen-ideal. Like Crane Williams finds love in man's "broken world" a "visionary company," an "instant in the wind" suffused with time's desperation. Blanche and Stanley become antiphonal figures in a choric exchange of ideas. The Freudian-Nietzschean paraphernalia operate in close conjunction as a massive assault on the futility of our civilized illusions, which Williams always portrays as both necessary and self-destructive.

The Apollonian-Dionysian motif is vigorously accentuated, but not exactly to Nietzsche's purpose. Blanche, as her name implies, is the pallid, lifeless product of her illusions, of a way of life that has forfeited its vigor through what she later calls her family's "epic fornications," perversions of a healthy procreative sex. Her "Belle Reve," the family plantation, rests in Apollo's orchard, "Laurel," Mississippi. She is in every sense the sum of an exhausted tradition that is the essence of sophistication and culture run down into the appearance that struggles to conceal rapacity. Her life is a living division of two warring principles, desire and decorum, and she is the victim of civilization's attempt to reconcile the two in a morality. Her indulgent past is a mixture of sin and romance, reality and illusion, the excesses of the self and the restraints of society. Williams has followed Nietzsche in translating what is essentially metaphysical hypothesis into a metaphor of psychological conflict. Her schizoid personality is a drama of man's irreconcilable split between animal reality and moral appearance, or as Freud put it figuratively, a mortal conflict of id against ego and superego. Blanche lives in a world of shades, of Chinese lanterns, of romantic melodies that conjure up dream worlds, of perversions turned into illusory romances, of alcoholic escape, of time past—the romantic continuity of generations to which she looks for identity—and of Christian morality that refines away, or judicially and morally vitiates, animal impulse. Thus, she is driven by guilt over the very indulgences that give Stanley's life a vital intensity.

As her anti-self, Stanley is as consciously created. Born under the sign of Capricorn, the Goat—as Blanche was born under the sign of Virgo—he is, according to the stage directions, a veritable Pan-Dionysus, the "gaudy seed-bearer," the embodiment of "animal joy" whose life "has been pleasure with women, the giving and taking of it, not with weak indulgence, dependently, but with the power and pride of a richly feathered male bird among hens." He is identified variously with the goat, the cat, and the locomotive, three rather obvious symbols that define his sex-centered life and repeatedly disturb Blanche's tenuous psychic balance. It is revealing, too, that Blanche very early sees in Stanley a source to reinvigorate the DuBois blood. This is no genetic plan but, on Blanche's part, a pathetic hope for the revival of the old dissipated values. She finds her evil lying in the blood and her values in the illusions which can explain away moral indiscretions. Those who acclaimed Williams's earthly Inferno mistook the symbolic scene for realism, failing to note the inverted image of a pagan Paradiso, where civilized values are in desuetude and the blood dictates a pulsating order of intensity and calm. The characters are to be judged, if at all, in degree to their response to the rhythm.

The love of Stanley for Stella describes precisely this rhythm of violence and reconciliation, and it exists beyond Blanche's ken. The jazz motif which alternates with the polka music—in contrast to Blanche's affinity for the romantic waltz—establishes the primitive norm to which each character adapts or suffers a dissonant psychic shock. All the old devices are here. The animal appetite is equated with the spiritual appetite for wholeness, and must be satisfied on its own terms, not those of a pre-established ethic. Stanley and Stella move freely between elemental sex and mystical experience, and Williams lends to their relationship every possible symbolic device to enforce the mystical oneness of their union. On the other hand, Blanche's neurotic reveries emerge from the internal drama of conflicting passions caused by her moral conscience. They are to be described, I suppose, in the familiar psychological terms of repression and transference, though the drama seems to lay the cause, not the cure, at the foot of consciousness and reason. Blanche's obsessive bathing is a nominal gesture of guilt and wished-for redemption, which becomes one of the play's recurrent symbols, along with the piano, locomotives, cats, telephones, and drink.

Alcohol plays a dual role. If it is one source of Blanche's hysterical escape from moral contingencies, it is likewise the stimulant of the Bacchic rites that punctuate Stanley's life. Drunkenness, indeed, is the physiological analogue for Dionysian ectasy, as the dream-illusion symbolizes the Apollonian state. Blanche drinks to induce illusion, to extirpate moral contradictions that stand between her and the pure "Belle Reve." But for Stanley, drink induces a state of conviviality and conjugal oneness that has meaning only because it is counterbalanced by violent disturbances of irrational passion. His moments of violence are caused invariably by an external intrusion into that oneness, though violence is an integral part of the blood rhythm by which he lives. The rape scene must be read in this context, even though it is popularly recorded as a combination of unremitting realism and over suggestive theatrics.

A closer look at a sequence of the play's middle scenes will, I think, underscore the way in which Williams exploits this primitive rhythm while moving his play along in temporal sequence. Scene 3 opens with some down-to-earth conversation at the poker table, set in the timeless impression of what the stage directions call a "Van Gogh" canvas. Blanche and Stella have gone out for dinner, a show, and drinks. They return soon after the scene opens, bringing into the masculine world a feminine interruption. Blanche's conduct is vulgarly suggestive, and a combination of her sexual gestures toward Mitch and her playing of the radio—first the derivative and conventionalized Latin rhythms of Xavier Cugat, then Viennese waltzes—leads conclusively to Stanley's violence upon Stella. The motivation here is not unsubtle. Stanley is incited to toss the radio out the window, and Stella responds with an uncharacteristic reproach: *"Drunk-drunk-animal thing, you!"* Stella for the moment echoes Blanche, judging her husband by the values of her old life, censuring the animal vitality that has rescued her from Blanche's effete world. The dramatic rhythm that completes the scene was the perfect opportunity for Brando's "method." Stanley's impulsive beating of Stella, her withdrawal, the moments of waiting while Stanley bellows goat-like in the wings, and the animal sensuality of their reconciliation fulfills the pattern of sexual will that concludes in a transcendental ecstasy of love. At the end Stella is once more within her husband's primitive embrace, to which she brings the spiritual, even cosmic, balance that his unformed vigor demands. But Blanche sees the whole affair only as "violence," upon her decorous sensibility and "Belle Reve." The real violence is the forced recognition of the conflicting drives within herself.

Scene 4 opens with the dramatic contrast between Stella and Blanche, the one "narcotized" like the face of an "Eastern idol," by her union of the previous night, the other pressed to the edge of anxiety. The entire scene is a drama of misunderstanding, accentuated by Blanche's wild but purposeless effort to rescue her sister, and thus the family, from animalistic forces. At one point she is driven to protest against Stella's mystical indifference to the night's affair by asking if her sister had cultivated a "Chinese philosophy," and one is not to miss the suggestion of identity between the Oriental calm and the sexual holiness of the two lovers. The scene moves through a series of neurotically aimless gestures on Blanche's part to a frenetic conclusion in her diatribe against an animalistic world. Immediately before the outburst, the cleavage between the two worlds is underlined:

> STELLA: But there are things that happen between a man and
> a woman in the dark—that sort of make everything else
> seem—unimportant. (*Pause*)
> BLANCHE: What you are talking about is brutal desire—just—
> Desire!—the name of that rattle-trap streetcar that bangs
> through the Quarter, up one old narrow street and down
> another . . .
> STELLA: Haven't you ever ridden on that streetcar?
> BLANCHE: It brought me here.—Where I'm not wanted and
> where I'm ashamed to be.

Love is the mystical leaven that for Stella—who, one presumes, is the ideal polarity of Stanley's realistic self—elevates the animal to the spiritual and makes them one. Uncomprehendingly, Blanche bursts out "plainly" against man's "anthropological" heritage, concluding her argument, that

Stella must join the legions of culture, with a revealing plea: "Don't—don't hang back with the brutes!" There is implicit in Blanche's remarks—made against the background of the inevitable train whistle, while Stanley stands in the wings—the call of history and progress, and the Apollonian illusion of reconciliation through culture, the arts, beauty. Against this rhetoric Williams juxtaposes the action of Stanley as a reminder of the necessary vitality in any creative dream, the incipient animal within the human. The conclusion of the scene once again resolves into the passionate order of sexual transcendence, leaving Blanche pathetically and helplessly within the hollow ring of her argument.

Scene 5 offers much of the same, with Blanche's quest for escape from reality played off against the fight between Steve and Eunice, which ends in a reconciliation of "goat-like screeches" while Blanche makes seductive gestures toward a bewildered newsboy under the illusion of medieval romance. And scene 6, after an interlude of Blanche's forced prudery to stave off Mitch and her own irrepressible desires, ends in a violent confession of her horror at the suicide of her homosexual husband. Confession here acts to release her momentarily into the ecstasy of union with Mitch, which in turn leads only in the subsequent scene to guilt, ritualistic bathing, and the intense clash of Stanley's brute truths about her past and Blanche's "make-believe" rationalizations. The structure of these scenes is sound and predictable, if not sensational. There is no act division in the play, perhaps because the theme disallows a syllogistic progression of human actions in time, while demanding a recurring pattern of conflict and reconciliation that accords with the natural rhythms of passion. Realistically viewed, Stanley's world is a dreadfully boring repetition of acts, but symbolically, it fulfills a timeless, ritualistic cycle. In a sense, the progressive action required by the play's realism is at odds with the archetypal inner action, which is no better revealed than in the contradictory function of the climax.

The rape that concludes scene 10 serves a double structural purpose of resolving that scene in a moment of passion and bringing the play to its climax. There is some confusion, however, between the rape as a plausible realistic act and as a symbolic ravishing of the Apollonian by the Dionysian self. For if the play's symbolic conflict is to be resolved, as is suggested by Stanley's cryptic statement to Blanche that "We've had this date with each other from the beginning," the final scene is not so clear in its implications. Blanche, in her psychologically ingrown virginity, is driven further into herself and her dream, not released, and is handed over to Williams's modern priest, the psychoanalyst, for care. There is an unclear mingling of themes here. Blanche at first withdraws from the doctor and matron—stereotyped, masculinized symbols of the state institution—only to capitulate to the doctor when he personalizes himself by removing his professional appearance. It is, then, suggested that Blanche is to be returned to the world, the one outside Stanley's and Stella's Elysium of mystical "love," where the necessity of illusion plays its ambiguous role. Stanley's act becomes in this context an egregious breach of morality—yet the play's conclusion obscures moral judgment.

Blanche, of course, comes to symbolize a civilized world that cannot face its essential and necessary primitive self, and thus exists in a constant state of internecine anxiety. Unlike suppliants of the Dionysian cult, she cannot devour the god whose self is the wafer of regeneration. And Williams offers, as he does elsewhere, the psychoanalyst as surrogate artist-priest, who must reconstruct the fragments of personality by absolving conflict and its attendant guilt. I hesitate to conceive Williams's conclusion in strict psychological terms, for he tempers psychoanalysis with a rather indeterminate mysticism. His analyst-priest is not the Freudian doctor whose purpose is to purge the irrational and reorient the self by making suppressed conflicts conscious and intelligible. This seems to be the human gesture of the analyst in *Suddenly Last Summer*, but even there Williams conceives of him as a kind of artist, remolding one personality out of the wasteful fragments of another. Williams indicates no clear trust in the rational solution. Blanche's fate and the future of her world remain ambiguous, but Stanley and Stella are reconciled by a dual motivation: Stella by the illusion that she must unquestioningly accept things as they are and not complicate them with moral suspicions; Stanley by an animal need that provides spiritual fulfillment. If the Dionysian self never senses conflict, he remains nevertheless a marginal figure, his ecstatic world beyond our realization. We are left with Blanche's pathos, and the ambiguous suggestions that through "love" she will be returned not to the emptiness of "Belle Reve" but to a civilized world of more substantial illusions. If she is the tragic victim of a world of unrestrained animal appetite, she must regain, even through compassion and understanding, some of the vitality (and thus the primitivism) exhausted by her heirs. And Stanley's world is left, in the play's concluding words, to repeat itself timelessly in a ritual of "seven-card stud," which must stand as a reproach to if not a solution for the etiolated rituals of a civilization that excludes the realities of the blood.

The confusions of *Streetcar* must be attributed, it seems to me, to three things: the play's insistence on an amoral scene, in which the Dionysian rhythm is retailed as a norm; the use of psychological motifs to authenticate primitivism; and the deliberate exploitation of intellectual themes and symbols in the cause of anti-intellectualism. Williams's rejection of contemporary civilization takes the easy form of repudiating the moral masks which suffocate natural man, but he in no way envisions the human tensions that Nietzsche found so integral to man's tragic dignity, nor does he offer in contrast a plausible antithesis to his rejection of civilization—except a vaguely subscribed "love." This is not to say that one should expect Williams to provide either moral or intellectual answers. But to offer the purely Dionysian as a primitive order beyond morality is essentially a negative commentary, even though Williams presumes to stress an innate good in vitalism. The dialogue that constitutes tragedy is stifled, and with it Blanche's cry.

Williams fabricates his Dionysian norm without the judicious insight he employed in *The Glass Menagerie*, where the individual rises above the world's decadence by coming to moral terms with himself and the bitter realities of that world. In the purely Dionysian world, as Nietzsche pointed out and as Williams fails to grasp, individuality must be sacrificed to the universal unconscious and the tensions of dramatic conflict dissolved into chaos. Dionysianism pure is chaos and not simply the primitive order suggested in the rise and fall of blood passions. Universal innocence forfeits moral judgment, for innocence is capable of the extremes of action (including both good and evil) and thus escapes morality. Williams disallows the moralist's conclusions against Stanley's world. It is amoral (primitive and thus chaotic and partial) but made whole at least through the spiritual complement of Stella. Her role, which seems to be defined with calculated purpose early in the play, never develops functionally, and her action in the final scene fails to clarify the play. This attenuation of Stella's role is a major factor in the play's unresolved conclusion. Thus, Stanley's unpalatable world is not to be seen as rapacious but as part of the essential and inescapable reality of things. What Williams misses, in attaching now a moral judgment, now symbolic innocence to his animal functionaries is that his final scene does insinuate moral predilections while the substance of the play has obviated the moral scene for the ritualistic. Blanche's world, our world, begs for sympathy in its very throes. Williams, having attended its funeral, is loath to depart the grave, for he discovers too late that he can return only to Stanley's virile but chaotic game. The play shocks not where it is supposed to—by a deft inversion of the prevailing norms, as in Gide's *The Immoralist*—but in its realism, which it does not successfully manage to suspend. *Streetcar* is torn asunder, like Orpheus by the Maenads, by overextended symbolism and an excess of self-consciousness. The simile is not altogether unrelated to Williams's total achievement.

ESTHER MERLE JACKSON

The Synthetic Myth

I say that symbols are nothing but the natural speech of drama.
—Preface to *Camino Real*

As Tennessee Williams has developed as a dramatist, he has become increasingly concerned about the limitations of a purely lyric form. In the preface to *Cat on a Hot Tin Roof* he records some of his reflections on this problem:

> The fact that I want you to observe what I do for your possible pleasure and to give you knowledge of things that I feel I may know better than you, because my world is different from yours, as different as every man's world is from the world of others, is not enough excuse for a personal lyricism that has not yet mastered its necessary trick of rising above the singular to the plural concern, from personal to general import. But for years and years now, which may have passed like a dream because of this obsession, I have been trying to learn how to perform this trick and make it truthful, and sometimes I feel that I am able to do it.

The playwright's problem is indigenous to the expressionistic forms. Indeed, his secondary motive—that of rising from the singular to the plural concern, from expression to meaning—has been voiced by many artists in the past half century. It was articulated as early as 1912 by Wassily Kandinsky and appeared in many of the later treatises published by artists in

From *The Broken World of Tennessee Williams.* © 1965 by Esther Merle Jackson. University of Wisconsin Press, 1965.

the Bauhaus School. Some of the concerns voiced by Kandinsky in his early essay *Concerning the Spiritual in Art* are recapitulated in Williams's statements:

> My own creed as a playwright is fairly close to that expressed by the painter in Shaw's play *The Doctor's Dilemma:* "I believe in Michelangelo, Velasquez and Rembrandt; in the might of design, the mystery of color, the redemption of all things by beauty everlasting and the message of art that has made these hands blessed. Amen."
>
> How much art his hands were blessed with or how much mine are, I don't know, but that art is a blessing is certain and that it contains its message is also certain, and I feel, as the painter did, that the message lies in those abstract beauties of form and color and line, to which I would add light and motion.

Williams echoes the interest of the expressionists in an "international state of art." For he suggests that the dramatic form, despite its individuality, must represent more than personal experience, that its contents must be somehow related to the collective consciousness. For Williams the problem of communication in the theater appears even more critical than comparable difficulties in the plastic arts. For the drama imposes a time limit on understanding. The playwright must articulate his work in such a way that the spectator may grasp its intent within the space of two hours. Moreover, the spectator must believe that his understanding is universal: that his knowledge links him with the whole of humanity, as well as with that particular audience with which he shares a momentary identity. He speaks of this quality of response in the preface to *The Rose Tattoo:* "For a couple of hours we may surrender ourselves to a world of fiercely illuminated values in conflict."

Williams recognized early in his career the need for a system of communication, for a theatrical language related specifically to the interpretation of reality in the modern world. The problem has its origin not only in the philosophical position of the dramatist, but also in the vastly extended knowledge of the twentieth century—a knowledge that has proliferated so rapidly it has outrun man's efforts to systematize it. The arts have continued to struggle with the problem of providing a comprehensive linguistic system for the vast accumulation of knowledge which is the legacy of the twentieth century. It is, declares Jean-Paul Sartre, the theater which must reassume the primary responsibility for defining, ordering, and interpreting truth. Williams's desire to discover universal meaning through drama assumes, in the context of this motive, even greater significance. The attempt to evolve a conventional system of understanding—a catalogue of common meanings—

for the drama looms as an undertaking of major importance, not only for this playwright but for the theater at large.

Francis Fergusson, in his exemplary study *The Idea of a Theater*, traces the drive toward the evolution of a modern theatrical language to Richard Wagner. Wagner attempted to establish for romantic drama a catalogue of symbols through which multiple contents could be given figuration. Fergusson traces Wagner's diagrammatic patterns to many sources: to the Olympian religions, to the iconography of Christianity, and to the imaginative traditions of Northern Europe. Fergusson observes that both the symbolists and the expressionists continued this search for representational systems which could mirror the complex modern consciousness. Some dramatists were successful in discovering such linguistic patterns on native grounds: the plays of Yeats, Synge, O'Casey, and Federico García Lorca are grounded in the poetic pasts of Ireland and Spain. Still other contemporary dramatists have used the linguistic apparatus of traditional Christian theology: plays such as Paul Claudel's *The Satin Slipper*, T. S. Eliot's *Murder in the Cathedral*, Christopher Fry's *The Boy with a Cart*, and, more recently, Jean Anouilh's *Becket*, Bertolt Brecht's *Galileo*, and John Osborne's *Luther* are partially dependent for their explications upon a language which has its roots in Christian thought and ritual.

The American dramatists have been deeply concerned with the problem of language, especially with the construction of symbolic forms. If Eugene O'Neill's early works such as *Marco Millions* (1923–25) employed a symbology frankly dependent on European sources, later works such as *Mourning Becomes Electra* (1931) were designed to exploit a pattern of expression which is in larger measure native. As a southerner, Tennessee Williams has had advantages of consequence: the symbolism of the South, a region separated from the mainstream of the American society by an intricate complex of political, cultural, and economic factors, has greatly enriched the language of the arts. The South, much of which retains many characteristics of primitive societies, has developed in its literature a conventional perspective described by some aestheticians as "southern agrarianism." Its primordial interpretation of man's struggle in an unfriendly universe has produced a highly developed iconography.

This southern aesthetic has provided for the drama of Williams a kind of basic linguistic structure comparable to that which appeared in elementary stages of Greek tragedy. For like the Greek myths, this southern apprehension has a socio-politico-religious grounding in a primitive society where the critical phases of the life struggle are interpreted in an intricate symbolic language. But while Williams employs the southern symbolism as one element of his syntax, he has attempted, especially in his later works, to progress from this elemental language to a more objective instrument of communication. His "Lord Byron" in *Camino Real* speaks of this process of transliteration:

> But a poet's vocation, which used to be my vocation, is to influence the heart in a gentler fashion than you have made your mark on that loaf of bread. He ought to purify it and lift it above its ordinary level. For what is the heart but a sort of—
> [*He makes a high, groping gesture in the air.*]
> —A sort of—*instrument!*—that translates *noise* into *music*, chaos into —*order* . . . —*a mysterious order!*
>
> (block 8)

As early as *The Glass Menagerie*, Williams began to create myths of modern life; that is, he began to weave the dark images of his personal vision together with certain sociological, psychological, religious, and philosophical contents, in a schematic explication of modern life. This activity, begun in his early work, was accelerated in middle plays such as *A Streetcar Named Desire, Summer and Smoke, Cat on a Hot Tin Roof, The Rose Tattoo*, and *Camino Real*. In these works, the playwright seems to have progressed to the creation of symbols of greater density, richer texture, and more comprehensive philosophical contents than those evident in his earlier plays. Williams comments on his attempt to evolve a more mature theatrical language:

> We all have in our conscious and unconscious minds a great vocabulary of images, and I think all human communication is based on these images as are our dreams; and a symbol in a play has only one legitimate purpose which is to say a thing more directly and simply and beautifully than it could be said in words.
> I hate writing that is a parade of images for the sake of images; I hate it so much that I close a book in disgust when it keeps on saying one thing is like another; I even get disgusted with poems that make nothing but comparisons between one thing and another. But I repeat that symbols, when used respectfully, are the purest language of plays. Sometimes it would take page after tedious page of exposition to put across an idea that can be said with an object or a gesture on the lighted stage.

Increasingly, the playwright has attempted to create a kind of ideograph in which form and content, feeling and meaning, understanding and reason are

wholly unified. Like Brecht, Williams conceives of a symbol so filled with
meanings that it embodies the whole of experience within its structural frame.
It is clear that one of the major difficulties which the playwright has faced
is the need for rational correlatives for personal experience. In *The Glass
Menagerie* Williams uses memory as a rationalizing ground, as a point of
reference around which his images are clustered. He has obviously found
the technique of recall useful; it has enabled him to exercise a high degree
of poetic selectivity as well as to defend that distortion which has been
necessary to the creation of his symbolic system. The memory device nevertheless has certain disadvantages; it embodies exactly the suggestion of personal limitation which the playwright wishes to transcend. In much of his
work, therefore, Williams has employed other devices, many of which are
associated with the practices of the surrealists.

In *A Streetcar Named Desire* and in *Summer and Smoke*, Williams creates
symbols which have as their rationale progressive insanity. Following André
Breton, Salvador Dali, and Giorgio de Chirico, he uses insanity, like intoxication and the dream, as a kind of instrumentation for the organization and
interpretation of experience. The insanity mechanism has advantages over
the device of memory, especially for works which have tragic implications,
for it suggests extremity in human circumstance. The prefrontal lobotomy
which threatens Catharine Holly in *Suddenly Last Summer* may thus be read
as the equivalent of classical "death." In the same way, the confinement of
Blanche to the asylum in *A Streetcar Named Desire* is a sign of annihilation as
final in its own way as the murder of Clytemnestra in the *Oresteia*. But the
use of the insanity device also presents certain dangers, not only as dem-
onstrated in the work of Williams and others in the contemporary group,
but also as seen in the work of traditional dramatists. The question of insanity
in *A Streetcar Named Desire* is, in this sense, an extension of a problem affecting
earlier plays, including *Orestes*, *Medea*, *Hamlet*, and *Miss Julie*. For with the
use of insanity as an interpretative instrument, the playwright risks invali-
dation of his vision. The modern spectator—at least at conscious levels of
response—feels himself the moral and intellectual superior of a deranged
protagonist. As a linguistic device in contemporary drama, however, insanity
is gaining validity. As the horrors of World War II have been exposed, the
effect of individual aberration on the course of human affairs has been doc-
umented by historical record.

Williams, however, has continued to search for other answers to the
problem of objectifying and validating his moments of critical insight. In
Cat on a Hot Tin Roof he explores the uses of a second scheme. He employs

in this play, as in *Sweet Bird of Youth*, another surrealistic device—intoxication. For Brick, truth exists in alcohol: it is alcohol which stops the flow of natural time and freezes the moment of experience in "metaphysical stasis":

> BRICK: I have to hear that little click in my head that makes me
> peaceful. Usually I hear it sooner than this, sometimes as
> early as—noon, but—
> —Today, it's—dilatory. . . .
> —I just haven't got the right level of alcohol in my
> bloodstream yet!
>
> (act 2)

Similarly, Alexandra del Lago, the fading movie queen of *Sweet Bird of Youth*, controls her perception of reality—her consciousness—by means of drugs. The decadent "Princess," a priestess in her own right, is the instrument through which the truth is revealed to the spectator as well as to the troubled protagonist Chance.

Williams makes some use of yet a third rationalizing apparatus: the dream organization, a pattern claimed by the surrealists but found throughout the work of Western dramatists. In the prologue to *Camino Real*, the desert rat "Don Quixote" speaks these explanatory lines:

> —And my dream will be a pageant, a masque in which old
> meanings will be remembered and possibly new ones discovered,
> and when I wake from this sleep and this disturbing pageant of
> a dream, I'll choose one among its shadows to take along with
> me in the place of Sancho.

We have noted [elsewhere] the dreamlike quality of Williams's visual imagination in the short work *This Property is Condemned*. His setting for *Summer and Smoke* is described in a similar way:

> Now we come to the main exterior set which is a promontory in
> a park or public square in the town of Glorious Hill. Situated
> on this promontory is a fountain in the form of a stone angel, in
> a gracefully crouching position with wings lifted and her hands
> held together to form a cup from which water flows, a public
> drinking fountain. The stone angel of the fountain should prob-
> ably be elevated so that it appears in the background of the interior
> scenes as a symbolic figure (Eternity) brooding over the course
> of the play. . . . I would like all three units to form an harmonious
> whole like one complete picture rather than three separate ones.

An imaginative designer may solve these plastic problems in a variety of ways and should not feel bound by any of my specific suggestions. . . .

Everything possible should be done to give an unbroken fluid quality to the sequence of scenes.

There should be no curtain except for the intermission. The other divisions of the play should be accomplished by changes of lighting.

Finally, the matter of music. One basic theme should recur and the points of recurrence have been indicated here and there in the stage directions.

(Production Notes)

In this sequence, then, poetic vision has been released from the restrictions of time, space, and causality. The same dream logic controls poetic vision in *Camino Real*. Williams, in this drama, has effected the kind of montage known to the dreaming mind—the metamorphosis of diverse times, places, and situations into the shape of a single figure, "Camino Real":

> *As the curtain rises, on an almost lightless stage, there is a loud singing of wind, accompanied by distant, measured reverberations like pounding surf, or distant shellfire. Above the ancient wall that backs the set and the perimeter of mountains visible above the wall, are flickers of a white radiance as though daybreak were a white bird caught in a net and struggling to rise.*
>
> *The plaza is seen fitfully by this light. It belongs to a tropical seaport that bears a confusing, but somehow harmonious, resemblance to such widely scattered ports as Tangiers, Havana, Vera Cruz, Casablanca, Shanghai, New Orleans.*
>
> (Prologue)

But if Williams is indebted to the surrealists for much of his language, he also employs in his work another kind of symbolic apparatus which may be traced to the scientific thinkers of the late nineteenth century. In *Cat on a Hot Tin Roof* he develops a kind of symbolism which is indebted to the great scientific naturalists, especially to Herbert Spencer and Charles Darwin. Williams interprets human existence as life in a great "zoo," a retrogressive step from the "glass menagerie." Big Daddy Pollitt describes humanity (act 2) in these naturalistic terms: "The human animal is a beast that dies but the fact that he's dying don't give him pity for others, no sir. . . ." In this work, Williams describes human existence in "biological" nomenclature. As he follows the example of the naturalists in positing biological existence as the fundamental "ground of reality," he is able to equate the loss of the procreative power as a sign of death. Similarly, he reveals the fate of Big Daddy Pollitt by showing his fearful deterioration as the victim of a corrosive disease.

This naturalistic symbolism permits Williams to conduct several kinds of explorations simultaneously. In *Cat on a Hot Tin Roof* he examines a social condition, reveals the inner life of the individuals who are affected, and shows the larger implications of the naturalist philosophy in the interpretation of the moral universe. The sickness of Brick therefore becomes the pivot for the penetration of an entire fabric of moral problems. Williams describes the protagonist's dilemma in this way:

> *The thing they're discussing, timidly and painfully on the side of Big Daddy, fiercely, violently on Brick's side, is the inadmissible thing that Skipper died to disavow between them. The fact that if it existed it had to be disavowed to "keep face" in the world they lived in, may be at the heart of the "mendacity" that Brick drinks to kill his disgust with. It may be the root of his collapse. Or maybe it is only a single manifestation of it, not even the most important. The bird that I hope to catch in the net of this play is not the solution of one man's psychological problem. I am trying to catch the true quality of experience in a group of people, that cloudy, flickering, evanescent—fiercely charged!—interplay of live human beings in the thundercloud of a common crisis. Some mystery should be left in the revelation of character in a play, just as a great deal of mystery is always left in the revelation of character in life, even in one's own character to himself. This does not absolve the playwright of his duty to observe and probe as clearly and deeply as he legitimately can: but it should steer him away from "pat" conclusions, facile definitions which make a play just a play, not a snare for the truth of human experience.*

>   (act 2)

With the aid of his biological symbology, Williams reconsiders a theme drawn from Greek tragedy. *Cat on a Hot Tin Roof* is a study of an extended cycle of human transgression. As Big Daddy Pollitt perceives the working out of the curse upon his house, he cries out, in Aeschylean tones, his malediction:

CHRIST — DAMN — ALL — LYING SONS OF — LYING BITCHES! . . . Yes, all liars, all liars, all lying dying liars! . . . —Lying! Dying! Liars!

                                                                        (act 2)

Of all Williams's plays, *Cat on a Hot Tin Roof* seems to have a movement most nearly like that of Greek drama. Its progression is, in many ways, tragic in kind. Williams indicates that he was conscious of this parallelism. The playwright suggests, however, that he was persuaded by the director to arrest the forward movement of the drama's tragic descent and to substitute for it a modified denouement. He describes the rationale which dictated this change:

> No living playwright, that I can think of, hasn't something valuable to learn about his own work from a director so keenly perceptive as Elia Kazan. It so happened that in the case of *Streetcar*, Kazan was given a script that was completely finished. In the case of *Cat*, he was shown the first typed version of the play, and he was excited by it, but he had definite reservations about it which were concentrated in the third act. The gist of his reservations can be listed as three points: one, he felt that Big Daddy was too vivid and important a character to disappear from the play except as an offstage cry after the second act curtain; two, he felt that the character of Brick should undergo some apparent mutation as a result of the virtual vivisection that he undergoes in his interview with his father in Act Two. Three, he felt that the character of Margaret, while he understood that I sympathized with her and liked her myself, should be, if possible, more clearly sympathetic to an audience.
>
> It was only the third of these suggestions that I embraced wholeheartedly from the outset, because it so happened that Maggie the Cat had become steadily more charming to me as I worked on her characterization. I didn't want Big Daddy to reappear in Act Three and I felt that the moral paralysis of Brick was a root thing in his tragedy, and to show a dramatic progression would obscure the meaning of that tragedy in him and because I don't believe that a conversation, however revelatory, ever effects so immediate a change in the heart or even conduct of a person in Brick's state of spiritual disrepair.
>
> However, I wanted Kazan to direct the play, and though these suggestions were not made in the form of an ultimatum, I was fearful that I would lose his interest if I didn't re-examine the script from his point of view. I did.

The change here is more than an alteration in stage directions. Insofar as this discussion is concerned, it represents a major adjustment in the cycle of action, an adjustment which moved the drama from its original position as a near-tragedy to a point in proximity to the thesis play of realist definition. For in terms of the symbolism to which Williams had committed himself in the early moments of the drama, there could have developed only complete and final catastrophe for the House of Pollitt.

Gradually, in his later works, Williams has put together a kind of modern myth, a symbolic representation of the life of man in our time. His myth is not an organic form; that is, it is not a fabric surfacing from the unconscious life of man, individual or collective. In this sense it differs from the great natural structures which have evolved through world religions and even from popular myths, such as those which now surround the figure of the legendary American cowboy. The contemporary myth of Williams is synthetic. It is composed, after the manner of cinematic montage, from the fragments of many ethical, philosophic, social, poetic, intellectual, and religious perspectives. But this synthetic structure must in this respect be accounted valid; for it is the image of modern man caught between opposing logics—man in search of a means of reconciliation. The myth of Williams mirrors modern man's dilemma—his need for a comprehensive system of interpretation, for a structure which can restore meaning to life and which can reconcile the conflict within reality itself.

In a seminar on *Camino Real* convened at Bochum, Germany, in 1953, some of the latent contents in Williams's myth were discussed at length. The scholars on that occasion identified his linguistic structure as expressionist in kind, but pointed out that his form has been clothed in symbolic contents which are specifically related to the "American imagination." They noted that Williams the observer, standing at midpoint in the twentieth century, has attempted in his work to represent all the forces, ideas, values, systems of thought, and modes of behavior which impinge upon the position of the American in our time. There appear to be three major schemata which provide a scaffold for this synthetic structure: the ritual myth of the theater, the literary myth of the twentieth century American, and the Freudian-Jungian myth of modern man.

Williams attempts to interpret vision with the help of an apparatus described by Fergusson as the *myth of the theater*. It was Nietzsche who rationalized Shakespeare's perception of the "world as theater," the "theater as world." Many contemporaries, including the existentialists, have pursued this line of reasoning and have suggested that the theater is the ground of ultimate reality, the instrument for discovering permanent truths. Williams employs this apprehension throughout his work. In *The Glass Menagerie* the protagonist articulates a proposition which reverses the normal order of reality by positing the stage as the ground of ultimate truth.

Throughout all of his work, Williams follows a plan which theatrical-izes—even ritualizes—ordinary experience. Consider this description from the short sketch *The Unsatisfactory Supper or The Long Stay Cut Short:*

> THE CURTAIN RISES *on the porch and side yard of a shotgun cottage in Blue Mountain, Mississippi. The frame house is faded and has a greenish-gray cast with dark streaks from the roof, and there are irregularities in the lines of the building. Behind it the dusky cyclorama is stained with the rose of sunset, which is stormy-looking, and the wind has a cat-like whine.*
>
> *Upstage from the porch, in the center of the side yard, is a very large rose-bush, the beauty of which is somehow sinister-looking.*
>
> *A Prokofief sort of music introduces the scene and sets a mood of grotesque lyricism.*
>
> *The screen door opens with a snarl of rusty springs and latches: this stops the music. . . .*
>
> *(The evenly cadenced lines of the dialogue between* BABY DOLL *and* ARCHIE LEE *may be given a singsong reading, somewhat like a grotesque choral incantation, and passages may be divided as strophe and antistrophe by* BABY DOLL'S *movements back and forth on the porch.)*

There is a similar ritualization of action in *Cat on a Hot Tin Roof.* The playwright's instructions for Maggie's opening soliloquy give some indication of this anti-realist approach:

> *In her long speeches she has the vocal tricks of a priest delivering a liturgical chant, the lines are almost sung, always continuing a little beyond her breath.*

In this drama, Williams has scored his record of suffering with the primitive incantations of children and servants:

> Skinamarinka–dinka–dink
> Skinamarinka—do
> We love you.
> Skinamarinka—dinka–dink
> Skinamarinka—do.
>
> (act 2)

Williams attempts to recover to the theater a primary article of faith, the primitive belief in the magical power of mime. In this and other works, he attempts to release his theater from realist restrictions and to reintroduce into the drama aspects of its original incantatory identity.

While Williams's symbols are to some degree indebted to the religious legends of the ancient Greeks and of the Northern Europeans, there are, woven into his myth of the theater, many figures drawn from Christian ritual. For Williams, like Shakespeare, is haunted with images of the suffering Christ. His works abound with symbols drawn from the passion plays: the *Redemption of Mary Magdalene; Christ before Pilate;* the *Crucifixion;* the *Descent from the Cross;* the *Harrowing of Hell;* and the *Sorrowing Mother of God.* Some of these figures may be seen in the verse play *The Purification.* Here Williams ritualizes a description of the murder of the girl Elena:

<blockquote>

RANCHER: Yes.
           I set up the ladder.

SON: Set up the steep, steep ladder—
           Narrow . . .

RANCHER: Narrow!—Enquiring
           If Christ be still on the Cross!   .

CHORUS: Cross!

SON: Against the north wall set it . . .

RANCHER: Set it and climbed . . .
           (*He clutches his forehead*). Climbed!

CHORUS: Climbed!

SON: Climbed!
           To the side of the loft
           that gave all things to the sky.
           The axe—
           for a single moment—
           saluted the moon—then struck!

CHORUS: Struck!

SON: And she didn't cry . . .

RANCHER: Struck!
           Aye, struck—struck—*struck!*

CHORUS: Struck!

(*Dissonant chords on the guitar, with cymbals. The two men surge together and struggle like animals till they are torn apart. There is a rumble of thunder.*)

</blockquote>

Another variation on the "crucifixion" theme appears in the final scene of *Orpheus Descending,* where the protagonist is incinerated with an acetylene torch:

VOICES OF MEN [*shouting*]:—Keep to the walls!
He's armed!
—Upstairs, Dog!
—Jack, the confectionery!
   [*Wild cry back of store.*]
Got him, GOT HIM!
—Rope, git rope!
—Git rope from th' hardware section!
—I got something better than rope!
—What've you got?
—What's that, what's he got?
—A BLOWTORCH!
—Christ . . .

(act 3, scene 3)

But Williams's exploitation of Christian mythology is more comprehensive than this use of symbolic motif. The Christian interpretation of the
life cycle is played over and over again in his drama. In his early works,
Williams's version of the Christian cycle is truncated. In *The Glass Menagerie*,
the playwright stops the movement of his progression of suffering and announces that the play, as yet without a philosophical resolution, is over. The
poet, in this early work, persuades the spectator to accept an aesthetic conclusion: the creation of the drama itself. In *A Streetcar Named Desire*, the cycle
of suffering does not progress to the point of clear resolution; Blanche "dies,"
and we are merely promised a new life in Stella's unborn child. In certain
of the later works, however, the spiritual renewal of the protagonist is completed. The gradual change reflected in Brick, like the enlightenment of the
priest Shannon in *The Night of the Iguana*, seems, however, to represent a
resolution which is primarily Christian rather than Greek in nature. Like
Shakespeare in *The Winter's Tale*, Williams attempts to transcend the tragic
effect of human action by superimposing an essentially Christian resolution. Like Leontes, his protagonist is redeemed by the power of human
compassion.

Intimately related to his apprehension of human action is the playwright's image of character. For Williams, man is the great sinner, the
transgressor against moral law. In his explication of the dilemma of modern
man, Williams is partially dependent on a fundamental and unsophisticated
theology. Like St. Paul, he views human existence as a condition necessarily
marked by unavoidable transgression. He draws man as a creature in need

of a mode of salvation, in search of a power which can transcend that vested in natural life. Like many orthodox Christian theologians, Williams defines this saving power as human love. It is not surprising that there appears throughout the fabric of his work much of the linguistic apparatus of Christian theology: especially its progression of sin, suffering, guilt, punishment, and expiation. Moreover, Williams prescribes a theological resolution for human suffering. He superimposes on his dark cycle of suffering a transcendent progression of love, sympathy, contrition, sacrifice, and understanding.

Through his rite of the theater, then, Williams plays out modern man's search for salvation. If he interprets the condition of man through this fundamental symbology, he also employs more sophisticated perceptions. Through his myth of the twentieth-century American, he attempts to relate many individually-oriented perceptions to the larger question of the destiny of civilization. Williams is especially concerned with the illumination of the role of the American in the world of the twentieth century. For this purpose he has had recourse to a technique employed by James Joyce, Ezra Pound, and T. S. Eliot. He has composed a "myth of human development" in which the milestones in man's progress—or retrogression—are marked by literary achievement.

Williams attempts to interpret the complex historical role of "the American" on the contemporary world stage. In each of his plays he describes a region of this native ground: St. Louis, New Orleans, the Delta, Glorious Hill, Mississippi, and an assortment of Central American towns. It is important to recognize that Williams's geography is essentially imaginative: the region of conflict which he symbolizes is the modern American mind. Beneath the personal accounts which form the bases of his dramas, there rages a critical struggle between ways of life. In *A Streetcar Named Desire* he polarizes this conflict in the school teacher Blanche, with her talk of poetry and arts, and the laborer Kowalski, with his life of animal joys. Blanche describes her antagonist in these terms:

> He acts like an animal, has an animal's habits! Eats like one, moves like one, talks like one! There's even something—sub-human—something not quite to the stage of humanity yet! Yes, something—ape-like about him, like one of those pictures I've seen in—anthropological studies! Thousands and thousands of years have passed him right by, and there he is—Stanley Kowalski—survivor of the stone age! Bearing the raw meat home from the kill in the jungle! . . . Maybe we are a long way from

being made in God's image, but Stella—my sister—there has been *some* progress since then! Such things as art—as poetry and music—such kinds of new light have come into the world since then! In some kinds of people some tenderer feelings have had some little beginning! That we have got to make *grow!* And *cling* to, and hold as our flag! In this dark march to whatever it is we're approaching. . . . *Don't—don't hang back with the brutes!*

(scene 4)

In *Summer and Smoke* the playwright continues his exploration of a major societal conflict. In this play, the protagonist Alma is described (scene 1) as a symbol of traditional humanist values: "She seems to belong to a more elegant age, such as the Eighteenth Century in France." It is in fact her disorientation from the contemporary world of Glorious Hill, Mississippi, which is the cause of Alma's destruction. In the end, it is the animalistic John Buchanan who—like Stanley Kowalski—conquers this representative of past civilizations. In certain later plays, Williams attributes successful conquest to his women. It is Maggie, for example, who lives and wins by the law of nature, as it is Alexandra del Lago in *Sweet Bird of Youth* and the widow Faulk in *The Night of the Iguana* who hold aloft the flag of the jungle. Through these representative characters, Williams explores the question of choice for civilization itself, a choice between past and present, between soul and body. If the myth of the theater interprets individual destiny in the moral universe, the myth of the American attempts to relate individual morality to societal conflict.

Perhaps the most familiar formation within Williams's linguistic structure is one that may be described as his *psychological myth*. So important has this structure been to the explication of the playwright's vision that it has often been interpreted as a primary element of his content. Although the boundary between form and content is exceedingly difficult to determine, it is an especially important distinction in the interpretation of Williams's work. For in the drama of Williams, the psychological myth is primarily linguistic in nature; that is to say, it attempts to determine how, not why, life occurs. Williams's psychological myth may be traced to many sources. While its immediate indebtedness to the researches of Freud is apparent, it illustrates clearly the dependence of Freudian theory on perceptions out of the Greek and Judaeo-Christian traditions. Indeed, many of the Christian apprehensions which the playwright employs find parallels in the schemata of Freud. For example, the triadic concept of reality associated with Christian theology has its counterpart in Freud's organization of the ego, super-ego,

and id. Moreover, Freud provides objective equivalents for the same phenomena which are given signification in the Christian cycle of sin-guilt-
expiation-catharsis. Both Christian mythology and the Freudian system—
like certain Greek apprehensions of the Olympian, Homeric, and Hellenic
periods—appear to be concerned with the same psychic phenomena.

Williams benefits from this pattern of correspondences in human apprehension and is able to exploit it in the construct of his own myth. For
he uses the Freudian language as a system for designating reality, its tripartite
divisions as signs of modes of experience, and its clinical nomenclature as a
description of universal human distress. David Sievers, in his study *Freud
on Broadway*, gives this explanation to Williams's use of sexual psychology
in *A Streetcar Named Desire:* "Williams arranges in compelling theatrical pattern the agonized sexual anxiety of a girl caught between *id* and *ego-ideal*."
Sievers is correct in his analysis; however, sexual anxiety in the theater of
Williams is a symptom of a more comprehensive form of despair. Its meaning
is grounded in the relationship of both Williams and Freud to larger patterns
in intellectual history. Williams, like Freud, establishes human personality
in its animal origins. For both, sexuality is the symbol of being. While later
thinkers in the psychological disciplines have tended to modify the rigid
system of early Freudian psychology, artists such as Williams have retained
much of this older language, primarily because it is easier to project than
the more abstract concepts such as social acceptance, the will-to-power, or
the will-to-meaning. Williams has taken his point of departure from a primitive interpretation of sexual anxiety as life anxiety. From this point of view,
it is possible to suggest that the dramatist, in all of his work, is concerned
with the same range of human problems that engage a large group of contemporary thinkers and artists.

Williams looks at man's inner life through his Freudian "glass," an
interpretative apparatus which has particular meaning in the tradition of
American letters. One of the most striking examples of his poetic use of this
language may be seen in his explication of crisis in *Cat on a Hot Tin Roof*.
This drama seeks to examine the condition of modern man through certain
perceptions associated with the naturalist philosophies of Darwin, Spencer,
Marx, and others. Such perceptions show man as an animal struggling for
supremacy, displaying the superiority of his will-to-live in a jungle filled
with other animals. But Williams also explores in this work the devastating
effect of unqualified acceptance of the naturalist ontologies. He projects above
his primary and secondary images yet a third image: a picture of humanity
characterized by growing despair, by the "sickness unto death." When Europeans such as Jean-Paul Sartre treat similar themes, they tend to define

them in philosophical, even ideological, terms. Such is the mode of treatment which Sartre accords his *Prisoners at Altona,* a portrayal of a family that has marked similarities to Williams's House of Pollitt. But while Sartre explains the decay of the German industrialist and his scions in philosophical and neopolitical terms, Williams describes the "Fall of the House of Big Daddy Pollitt" in the language of Freud.

In *Cat on a Hot Tin Roof,* then, sexual failures are but the outer sign of inner disaster. For the true themes of the drama are metaphysical loneliness, nausea, and despair. Williams describes these stages in the existential progression in clinical language. He connotes Brick's loneliness—his alienation from friend, wife, father, mother, and God—through a series of clinically described symptoms. He describes his nausea through his lack of interest in all human relations. He defines his dread in a classically composed pattern of vacillation, from impotence to overcompensation. Williams interprets the crisis in this play as Brick's failure to understand the nature of his own existence—a failure which the playwright describes as "latent homosexuality." Despite the nature of the communicative structure employed, the main theme of the play is not sexual anxiety. *Cat on a Hot Tin Roof,* according to Williams's own definition, is a study of "mendacity," an image of falsity in life. Williams's protagonist suffers from "the sickness unto death," from that despair born of transgression, guilt, and alienation.

The British critic E. Martin Browne comments on this play in the preface to an English edition:

> To an Englishman, he opens a vision of the size of America, the huge fertility which can place apparently inexhaustible power in a man's hands . . . "twenty-eight thousand acres of the richest land this side of the valley Nile." Big Daddy is a patriarch: he reminds one of a character in Genesis (perhaps from the less frequently quoted chapters); he has the same warmth of the soil in him. The best poetry of the play is in his speeches, which distil the wisdom of primitive human nature.
>
> Brick and his Cat, the centres of the drama, vibrate in their desperation with the heat of the South. The family is clothed with the atmosphere of the South as with a garment. It is caged in the hot, thin-walled house, a prison amid the vast, rich lands around it. Tennessee Williams's use of repetition to create a prison of words is extraordinarily skilful: words beat like a tattoo on the heart, yet the beat is subtly changed at each hearing. This evocative quality of rhythm again reminds one of Synge. Perhaps it

is no accident that in both writers the quality springs from a sad
soil. . . .

American drama, as it comes to maturity, enlarges the horizons
of the theatre.

Williams approximates, in this modern myth, the Greek horror of crime
against life. Brick, like Oedipus the King, is a man guilty of a crime, a
transgression so dread that neither he nor his family dare to speak its name.
Williams finds in homosexuality an equivalent for the Greek sin of incest.
Through this parallel, he is able to illumine a pattern of correspondences
between that archaic civilization and our own.

A close study of Williams's use of psychology shows that the playwright
has modified the rigid structure of the early Freudian system with other
related perspectives, the most important of which is the poetic construct of
Carl Gustav Jung. For Williams, Jung's theories meet certain problems for
which the Freudian orthodoxy does not provide explication. The most obvious of these necessary arrangements is Jung's theory of image-making: his
concept of primordial and archaic forms written in the collective unconscious.
This theory, basically that cited by Williams in his own discussion of image-
making, has been extremely useful to a large group of contemporary artists
who have required a way of rationalizing their own perceptions.

Perhaps the chief value of Jung to Williams and others is the kind of
poetic ambiguity embodied in his theory of images. Jung wrote in a discussion
of poetic types,

> The great problems of life . . . are always related to the primordial
> images of the collective unconscious. These images are really
> balancing or compensating factors which correspond with the
> problems life presents in actuality.
>
> This is not to be marvelled at, since these images are deposits,
> representing the accumulated experience of thousands of years of
> struggle for adaptation and existence. Every great experience in
> life, every profound conflict, evokes the treasured wealth of these
> images and brings them to inner perception; as such, they become
> accessible to consciousness only in the presence of that degree of
> self-awareness and power of understanding which enables a man
> to think what he experiences instead of just living it blindly. In
> the latter case he actually lives the myth and the symbol without
> knowing it.

Unlike Freud, Jung considers, in his system, all aspects of human experience,
even those phenomena for which he can offer no scientific explanation:

> I can only gaze with wonder and awe at the depths and heights
> of our psychic nature. Its non-spatial nature conceals an untold
> abundance of images which have accumulated over millions of
> years of living development and become fixed in the organism.
> My consciousness is like an eye that penetrates to the most distant
> places, yet it is the psychic non-ego that fills them with non-
> spatial images. And these images are not pale shadows, but tre-
> mendously powerful psychic factors. The most we may be able
> to do is misunderstand them, but we can never rob them of their
> power by denying them.

Jung's system is a more flexible and indeed a more poetically conceived
schema than that of the scientist Freud. While Jung has attempted in his
work to systematize human experience and to submit human personality to
scientific scrutiny, his psychology retains a poetic ambiguity—a recognition
of the impenetrability of those aspects of experience which Wagner described
as "unknowable." His theory of the collective unconscious, with its roots in
racial memory, provides therefore an epistemology consistent with the poetic
interests of Williams.

A second advantage for Williams lies in Jung's eclecticism, in his ability
to synthesize a large group of perceptions relevant to the life of Western
man. In his theory of archetypes, Jung provides a symbolic structure that
is concerned with the meaning of the whole pattern of Western history:
cultural, political, social, and intellectual. Williams finds an appropriately
poetic symbol for human experience in Jung's concept of the "human
odyssey," the journey toward understanding. But while Jungian psychology
takes account of a universe in conflict—the broken world of Williams's description—its essentially aesthetic view of experience provides hope of individual reconciliation. If Williams borrows from Freud his apparatus for
the description of suffering humanity, he gains from the construct of Jung
justification for his hope of salvation. For Jung, like Williams, offers art as
the chief instrument of human reconciliation:

> Nobody can stand the total loss of the archetype. When that
> happens, it gives rise to that "frightful discontent in our culture,"
> where nobody feels at home because a "father" and "mother" are
> missing. Everyone knows the provisions that religion has always
> made in this respect. Unfortunately there are very many people
> who thoughtlessly go on asking whether these provisions are
> "true," when it is really a question of a psychological need. Noth-
> ing is achieved by explaining them away rationalistically.

Jung confirms Williams's belief that the great conflicts of life are made whole as images:

> Eternal truth needs a human language that alters with the spirit of the times. The primordial images undergo ceaseless transformation and yet remain ever the same, but only in a new form can they be understood anew. Always they require a new interpretation if, as each formulation becomes obsolete, they are not to lose their spellbinding power. . . . Where are the answers to the spiritual needs and troubles of a new epoch? And where the knowledge to deal with the psychological problems raised by the development of modern consciousness? Never before has "eternal" truth been faced with such a hybris of will and power.

In Jung's poetic image of the odyssey—the journey toward meaning, the search for self and soul—Williams finds a symbol for the reality of his description. Moreover, he finds in Jungian theory justification for his belief in art as a mode of transcendence, as a reconciling symbol in which the conflicts of life may be effectively resolved.

It is, then, this synthetic myth—a structure consciously composed from diverse moral, intellectual, social, political, and symbolic perspectives—which is one of the major characteristics of the theater of Tennessee Williams. Although European dramatists have themselves devised such an eclectic construct, they have used, in the main, philosophical, literary, and ideological perceptions as the raw materials of their myths. Jean-Paul Sartre has written that French dramatists have eschewed biological and psychological explications of reality because of their grounding in the limited apprehensions of the nineteenth-century naturalists. Americans have, on the contrary, employed perceptions which reflect the bias of a somewhat different heritage.

As Williams has succeeded in familiarizing his audiences—and his interpreters—with his conventional system of explication, many of the latent meanings of his work have come into view. Despite the effectiveness of his myth, the drama of Williams has retained, nonetheless, a fundamental inner division: an antagonism between feeling and reason, expression and meaning. For the process of synthesis has not yet been completed. Although Williams has gained from many sources—including the structures of Carl Gustav Jung—support for his system-building, his work has not yet overcome the fundamental problem of the modern arts: the evolution of a truly effective mode of aesthetic transcendence. There remains within the structural form— if not in the vision itself—an inorganicism, a critical tension between motion and arrest, the concrete and the abstract, experience and art.

LEONARD QUIRINO

Tennessee Williams's Persistent Battle of Angels

When Tennessee Williams published the text of *Orpheus Descending* which, in its first incarnation on Broadway in 1957 had lasted only sixty-eight performances, he included in the same volume the play on which it was based, *Battle of Angels*, which had opened in Boston in 1940 and had never reached Broadway at all. Read together, the two plays reveal a highly respectable reason for their commercial and aesthetic failure: the author's frantic ambition to make each of them a compendium of almost everything he believed about life and its artistic reflection in drama. In each of the plays, Williams attempted to amalgamate tragedy (both Greek and domestic), melodrama (both metaphysical and psychological), morality play (both frankly allegorical and subtly symbolic), ritualistic drama (with overt and covert mythic referents) and romantic mood play (both visually and verbally poetic). Each of the plays thematically attempts to depict sexual repression as the basis of religious sublimation and social hypocrisy, to portray the inability of love and sex to counteract God-given aloneness, and to sketch a portrait of the life and fate of the artist as a pariah-scapegoat in quest of meaning in a waste land. Above all, each of the plays attempts to celebrate existence as a continuous battle of the forces of light against those of darkness in which the former, though cruelly defeated (often by mutiny within their own ranks) are never totally destroyed though they appear never destined to win.

Compared with *Battle of Angels*, *Orpheus Descending* reveals Williams's greater control of the dramatic effects of image and symbol, his gain in

From *Modern Drama* 11, no. 1 (May 1968). © 1968 by the University of Toronto, Graduate Centre for the Study of Drama.

confidence in the audience's ability to recognize thematic patterns without
blunt and excessive signposts and his diminished need to rely too heavily on
melodramatics to convey his vision of tragedy. The earlier play, however,
because of its very bluntness provides an excellent blueprint to Williams's
sexual, social and religious or cosmic attitudes as they have persisted with
little modification to the present day. Furthermore, a close reading of *Battle
of Angels* reveals Williams in the act of grappling to find suitable dramatic
metaphors to express his basically abstract concerns and insights.

Because throughout *Battle of Angels* Williams uses verbal and theatrical
imagery that demands moral interpretation in universal terms, it becomes
imperative from the first to consider even what appears to be the play's most
realistic details as part of its predominantly symbolic design. That the play
is less concerned with the plight of some unfortunate people existing in the
Deep South than in the plight of existence itself becomes immediately apparent when the stage setting is examined as part of the whole moral-symbolic
context which it introduces.

The setting of *Battle of Angels* is conceived as *"A 'mercantile' store in a
very small and old-fashioned town in the Deep South."* Considered in context of
those elements which make *Battle of Angels* a morality play, that this great
stage of fools is portrayed as a store bears out the view expressed throughout
the drama that the buying and selling not only of goods but of human beings
is one of the primary social ills of the human condition. This store which
is the domain of Jabe Torrance, who is compared to "the very Prince of
Darkness," *"has large windows facing a tired dirt road"* (what else but the road
of life?) *"across which is a gasoline pump,* [and] *a broken-down wagon"* (possibly
reflecting the necessity and impossibility of physical and spiritual pilgrimage
on that road *"and cotton fields which extend to a cypress brake"* (the cemetery in
the play is called Cypress Hill) *"and the levee"* (or the bank of the river which
is the source of life). Considered in terms of the myth of Orpheus which
permeates the play, the setting suggests the kingdom of Hades and the river
not only the source but the end of life, the Styx. The interior of the store,
Williams tells us, is *"dusky"* and, in the epilogue which takes place on the
same set, that it resembles a *"pillaged temple."* Since it is the home and store
of Jabe who, in the Manichean conflict posited in the play symbolizes death,
destruction and the jealous god of darkness, its windows (metaphysical out-
look) are *"shielded from sunlight"* (the kingdom of natural law and light) and
its own lighting fixtures (source of illumination or doctrine) are *"old-fashioned"*
(outworn and perhaps indestructible). In line with this interpretation, it is
interesting to note that in the last act when Jabe and the powers of darkness
seem to be conquering the forces of light, the electricity in the town fails

completely due to the storm which is symbolically identified by Cassandra as "A battle in heaven. A battle of *angels* above us!" and the town and store are plunged into darkness and chaos. Also part of this interior, at the foot of the stairway leading to Jabe's quarters above, is the store's *"confectionery department"* which is the favorite province of Jabe's wife, Lady Torrance, who by art and imagination will make it an embodiment of the dream and memory of happiness, a temporary escape from the harsh reality of which it is a part.

Besides resembling a pillaged temple, the interior represents also a tragic *"Museum exhibiting souvenirs of the sensational events which had taken place there. Various articles connected with the tragedy are on display, such as the snakeskin jacket, which is suspended in a conspicuous position."* This snakeskin jacket which belonged to the poet, Val Xavier, the foe of the god of darkness and repression, represents, like the archetypal serpent itself, revolt, insidious knowledge and wisdom, physical rebirth (since traditionally the serpent casts its slough and grows young again) and an eternal and dangerous force in a creation that is, if anything, even more venomous than itself. As the curtain rises on the prologue, we see the Conjure Man dozing in a chair of this temple-museum; he is an ancient, cadaverous, wizard-like Negro who is like a watchman of the night and of the demonic forces of existence. It was he who became custodian of the snakeskin jacket when Val Xavier was captured and he who held it aloft as a banner of "the Beast Untamed" and "A souvenir of the jungle!" which remains "fresh and clean" when "Other things get dusty."

The prologue takes place a year after the tragic events which, in flashback, constitute the main action of the play. Jabe's store-museum-temple is now supported by the community and ministered by the Temple sisters who act as chorus to the tragedy, guides to the museum and vestal virgins of the temple. Typical busybody, altar-guild spinsters, the Temple sisters are portrayed as handmaidens of a cruel god whom they can never comprehend except as he touches some secret, vicious chord of their frustrated lives. Their militant and Pharisaic "Christianity" together with their admission charge of twenty-five cents per person for those who may wish to view the relics of the tragedy in the temple-museum constitute Williams's satirical view of organized religion as it thrives on a sanctified sensationalism which it totally misinterprets and which it propagates, ironically, as a testament to the dark deity's justice, righteousness and love.

The day on which the action in the prologue takes place is Sunday. Two tourists are being shown through the museum-temple, as is the audience, by the Temple sisters who comment on the tragic events of the previous year—now become almost epic and mythic—to which the place is a memorial. As the Temple sisters chorically discuss these events which are highly charged with religious symbolism, the action itself begins to unfold in flashback as though kindled by the Sunday performance-services of the two old ladies. The sound of a gong ends the last act and a religious chant at the close of the epilogue ends the play. The main action, therefore, may be viewed as a kind of ceremony—both theatrical and religious—within the choric framework of prologue and epilogue. That the events are thus capable of ceremonial recreation may signify, as do the events of Tom's memory in *The Glass Menagerie*, their continuing psychological relevance and life. Also, this manner of recreation signals the audience to consider the symbolic rather than merely the local-color aspects or verisimilitude of the main action.

Twice in the stage directions for the setting Williams uses the term "tragedy" to describe what he calls also the "sensational events" which constitute the action of the play. If this action is what Williams considers tragic, then his tragic vision could be said to consist, in part at least, of the spectacle provided by the battle of the forces of life against those of death as they manifest themselves physically, psychologically, sexually, morally, socially, in religion and in the role and fate of the artist. Williams portrays this battle of light and dark "angels" as tragically doomed since the struggle is unequal; the forces of life themselves—and this is the darkest, most despairing aspect of his vision—contain mutinous, life-denying elements within their own ranks and composition. For example, the "prophetess" in the play, Cassandra Whiteside, is counselled by the dead from their grave to "*live!*," a philosophy which she frantically preaches, but her own psychological constitution and impulses to destructiveness make her life catastrophic, and the abandonment to hedonism and to "jooking" which she interprets their exhortation to mean proves only self-defeating in practice. In Williams's tragic vision, the hero appears to be the person who attempts to defy the common tragic fate, the inbuilt obsolescence of anything that exists in time. Quixotically, he or she tries—as lover, artist or visionary—to achieve, fulfill or memorialize the ideal which Williams believes is occasionally perceptible but which, by definition, is beyond the grasp of imperfect mortality. Williams portrays his protagonists as pilgrims of the absolute who, setting forth on the road to the temple of Eros are beseiged from within or destroyed from without by the more powerful forces of Thanatos.

In *Battle of Angels*, Williams presents the forces of life and death in various fusions, combinations and battles. He portrays death in the figure of Jabe who, himself dying of cancer, is united in a loveless, barren marriage with life in the person of Myra. In the course of the play, Myra conceives a child by the continually pursued force of Eros embodied in the young poet who is named Val Xavier (a name suggesting the martyred St. Valentine as "love-saviour"). Val has formerly called himself Jonathan West (combining the Hebrew name meaning "the Lord has given" with, possibly as direct object, the point of the compass often used poetically to symbolize death). Protagonist Val, antagonist Jabe and complicating catalyst Myra form the basic triangle of the romantic element of the plot. Val's and Myra's child, the living product of two forces which attempt to defy and to transcend death, is never born; its parents are both destroyed by Jabe and his minions.

The action-packed catastrophe of this tragic play is partially redeemed from what appears to be gratuitous melodrama if we keep in mind the symbolic significance of the characters forming the triangle. Jabe is the most simply conceived of them because his dedication to destruction is whole-hearted and inflexible; his only purpose in prolonging his life is to make certain that life will not survive him; when he fires at Val he kills, instead, Myra who is hysterically accusing Val of "robbing the store" (*i.e.*, the sham life or living death that she had settled for). Myra falsely accuses Val of robbery in order to frighten him into remaining with her, but Val selfishly prefers his own freedom to her selfish desire of binding him to her death-in-life. Myra, more or less the Eurydice to Val's Orpheus throughout, becomes in the end another destructive bacchante when he refuses to rescue her immediately from the lord of the netherworld, Jabe-Pluto, to whom she had previously surrendered herself. Though she repudiates Jabe's destructive methods Myra finds, in her hysteria, that she is incapable of transcending them. Where Williams fails at the end is in crossing his cleverly conceived adaptation of the Orpheus-Eurydice myth of life, death and love with a fuzzily conceived version of the Christian story of Easter in which Jabe as Jehovah or God the Father demands the death of Val, the scapegoat and redeeming Christ-figure. Myra, here, is presumably to be interpreted as Mary, the virgin bride of God the Father and the mother of Christ, who protests the Lord's destruction of her earthly son. But what, except incest, are we to make of the carnal love affair between Val-Christ and Myra-Mary? Through lack of control, Williams's symbolic referents become unintelligible.

Even apart from whatever role she may have in the Easter motif of the play, the figure of Myra Torrance appears to be one of the most complex elements in the symbolic composition of *Battle of Angels*. Besides occasionally suggesting the imprisoned Eurydice waiting to be rescued by Val-Orpheus, in her unhappy marriage to Jabe-Pluto and her concern with barrenness and fertility she suggests Persephone. Like this goddess of the netherworld who slumbered fitfully in the winter, Myra Torrance when we first meet her is unable to sleep: we see her calling the drugstore in the middle of the night to ask for Luminal sleeping tablets. We see her, also, importing her "spring line" of goods. When we last see Myra, it is spring and she is pregnant with Val's child. The name that Jabe gave her in marriage suggests the torrents of the Styx—or of the river which, flooded by the storm at the climax of the play, prevents Val's escaping her hell.

Possibly even more complex and certainly more paradoxical is the figure of Val Xavier. Not only does he represent the martyred force of life and love as his name suggests but he is presented also as a faun-like creature who denies his eroticism and resents being considered a "male at stud"; as a wanderer in quest of the meaning of life who yet seeks rest and stability; and in opposition to Jabe, as a force of light who, at the same time, is no stranger to the creative aspect of the dark forces, the "Beast Untamed," inherent in nature. He compares himself to a fox and he is not only literally pursued by hounds but also figuratively hounded by sex-envy, social conformity, and hypocrisy. At the same time, Myra notes his resemblance to the hounds themselves: *"Who are you?"* she asks. "My God, you got eyes that shine in the dark like a dog's." This use of paradoxical and ambivalent symbolism accords with the dualism, self-opposition, and fatal self-destructiveness which Williams dramatizes throughout the play. The fox in the man attempts to escape the pursuing dogs by leading them to a dead end. Most paradoxical of all is Williams's portrayal of Val as a Christ-figure. Like Faulkner's analogy of Joe Christmas with Christ in *Light in August*, Williams's analogy is based not on sanctity or godliness, but on the sacrificial aspect of Christ as scapegoat. Since Christ is a symbolic referent so special in denotation and rich in connotation its analogical use in creative writing may be, categorically, ill-advised; however, as a short-cut to effecting audience sympathy for victims its continued popularity is assured. Presented with a Christ-figure, what we are expected to judge is not the worthiness of that fictional character to represent Christ; rather, we are expected to judge ourselves by the harshness or sympathy which we accord the author's representative of Christ-as-scapegoat be that figure ever so amoral in terms of conventional Christianity. In the case of Val Xavier we are presented with the aspect of the Messiah as love-god opposing a Pharisaical view of Jehovah as a jealous God of Wrath. Or more nearly, we are presented with a Christ-figure who, in his energy, rebelliousness, and love of freedom, is cast in the romantic, Blakean mold of Christ as Orc, an artist who is a member of the devil's party opposed to the tyrannical father-figure of Urizen. If we look any further into our knowledge of myth, of the New Testament, or of literature in an attempt to interpret Williams's symbolic design of Val Xavier more specifically we should, I fear, only confuse the interpretation of contextual symbols.

Two major characters whose relationship to the basic triangle is peripheral are Cassandra Whiteside and Vee Talbott. They are woven into the design of the play primarily by means of their relationship to Val as he embodies the doomed life force. Both ladies are visionaries of sorts, though each uses different, traditionally opposite means for trying to spell out the significance of existence. Cassandra who considers sensual pleasure and sexual gratification the only intimations of immortality which humans are suffered is obsessed with Val's body; passion, for her, is "the only one of the little alphabet blocks they give us to play with that seems to stand for anything of importance." Vee Talbott, an ascetic who is given to hallucination and who is subject to religious visions is intent on saving Val's soul; she is completely unaware of her sexual frustration and of the sexual imagery (such as the huge red steeple dominating the painting she makes of her church) which her "primitive" art works betray. Each of these ladies identifies Val as one of her own kind: Cassandra focuses on his wildness, rootlessness and individuality as the essence of her kinship with him, Vee on what she considers his Christ-like purity and gentleness. Neither lady is capable of seeing beyond the projection of her own needs, and each of them, though unintentionally, becomes in her devotion to him, as responsible for his death as the frenzy of the bacchantes was responsible for the dismemberment of Orpheus. Both Cassandra and Vee, like Val, are considered eccentric *persona non grata* in the dark, mercantile world. Cassandra cannot conquer her own death instinct which she believes proceeds from the fatality of her heredity and environment. She says to Val:

> I felt a resemblance between us. . . . You—savage. And me—
> aristocrat. Both of us things whose license has been revoked in
> the civilized world. Both of us equally damned and for the same
> good reason. Because we both want freedom. . . . I'm rotten.
> Neurotic. Our blood's gone bad from too much interbreeding.
> They've set up the guillotine, not in the Place de Concorde, but
> here, inside our own bodies!

Vee, significantly, is married to the sheriff who is in league with the powerful Jabe and instrumental in Val's destruction; neither through vision or sublimation can she transcend her involvement with the forces of death. In the epilogue to the play, we learn that Vee Talbott has lost her mind and that, accidentally or not no one knows, Cassandra has drowned.

Clearly, from the way Williams has designed the situations and subjected his characters to the inexorable outlines of various myths—all tragic myths except for the redemptive Easter one which in context makes a minimum of sense—we see that in *Battle of Angels* he is intent on portraying the impossibility of satisfactory exit from the existential situation of hell on earth. Like the hell of Sartre's *No Exit*, the hell of *Battle of Angels* consists, to a great extent, of the nausea which man collaborates in effecting by the relationship he sustains with himself and others; unlike the horrors of "hell" posited in Sartre's philosophy and in *The Flies*, however, the horrors of Williams's hell are not capable of being outfaced by the extraordinary exercise of human will and reason. Though Williams portrays his protagonists as attempting to escape the psychological prisons of heredity and environment, he shows that these bars are not pregnable to the realization of bad faith and the resolution to create one's own life. If, again, we disregard the poorly integrated use of the Easter myth whose implications of eternal salvation Williams appears to have ignored just as Sartre ignored in *No Exit* the heaven which the existence of his hell implied, we may say that the plight of Williams's characters is even more desperate than that of Sartre's. Any attempt at seeking some measure of fulfillment in existence is portrayed as doomed to failure in *Battle of Angels*.

The similarity between *No Exit* (1944) and *Battle of Angels* is coincidental (there is no question of direct influence) and I introduce the comparison primarily to highlight the contrasting visions and theatrical expressions of two contemporary dramatists who have portrayed hell as a metaphor for existence. Whereas Sartre's characters are being punished for cause, Williams's protagonists are essentially innocent victims of human, divine, and absurd tyranny. And while Sartre's play is a tightly constructed, elegant, chilling, psychological-philosophical *drame a thèse*, Williams's is a poetic, operatic, vocative celebration of the demonic powers of darkness. The basic animus of Sartre's work is rational, of Williams's it is emotional. Yet Williams's play is not entirely without systematic thought.

The "exits" or possibilities for transcending the limitations of existence which Williams's explores in *Battle of Angels* are love and sex, religion and art. While the chaotic powers of darkness are portrayed as ultimately victorious, Williams shows that momentary breakthroughs of light, though they may reveal only the extent of the darkness, are possible.

I have already mentioned Cassandra's belief that passion offers the only alphabet blocks with which we may hope to learn how to spell out the meaning of existence. The irony of her holding this belief, however, must also be noticed. In addition to portraying Cassandra's instinct for self-destruction (the relationship between death and sex in this play is as pronounced as it is in Elizabethan drama), Williams portrays her incapacity for sexual fulfillment. Physically, sex is incredibly painful for her: "Look at my wrists," she says. "They're too thin. You could snap them like twigs. You can see through my skin. It's transparent like tissue paper. I'm lovely, aren't I? But I'm not any good." While the consequences of this fragility are only hinted at in *Battle of Angels*, their meaning is spelled out in *Orpheus Descending* when Carol Cutrère, the character based on Cassandra Whiteside says: "The act of love-making is almost unbearably painful, and yet, of course, I do bear it, because to be not alone, even for a few moments, is worth the pain and the danger. It's dangerous for me because I'm not built for childbearing." The implication is obvious: the sexual key to meaning may be incapable of being put to use.

If we find Cassandra's case too special to be universally representative, we are offered in Carol's speech an implication about sexual communion which is developed in both plays and which is not to be disregarded as freakish: the fact of human aloneness. A major theme of both plays concerns the existential solitude of incarnation. Val says to Myra at one point: "We're all of us locked up tight inside our own bodies. Sentenced—you might say— to solitary confinement inside our own skins." To substantiate his claim to the truth of this assertion, Val offers the proof of his first experience of love which Williams portrays in idyllic terms not entirely devoid of images of death (the bed of love is made of cypress and moss). As a boy of fourteen, when Val had thought that he might literally absorb the meaning of the universe through his pores and senses from the "blazing . . . sunlight" he met a young girl the love of whom he was tempted to think constituted the meaning he was seeking. "When I was with her," he tells Myra, "I quit thinking because I was satisfied with just that; that sweetness between us, the long afternoons on the moss. But when I'd left her, the satisfaction would leave me and I'd be . . . like this. [*He clenches his fist.*] Right on the edge of something tremendous. It wasn't her. She was just a woman, not even a woman quite, and what I wanted was . . ." "Was *what?*" Myra asks. "Christ," Val answers, "I don't know. I gotta find out." Is "Christ" meant to be direct object as well as expletive? Probably. At any rate, Williams has Val rule out his experience of love as an exit out of meaninglessness. Indeed, Val thinks of his first love as "waitin' for . . . a kind of a signal—to *trap* me" and this foreshadows his reaction to Myra's love for him later. For the paradoxical fact of human existence which Williams is celebrating is that while man laments his loneliness he is equally drawn to the freedom of solitude or *chosen* aloneness. When Myra joyously informs Val that she is bearing his child, she says "So now you see we can't be separated! We're bound together, Val!" Val recoils from her, "Bound? No! I'm not bound to nothing! Never could be, Myra." Then Myra compares herself to the "woman from Waco,"

the fury who claimed that Val wooed and jilted her and who then hounds
him to his death. Indeed, far from providing existential salvation, love is
fatal for Val. He interprets the love which the woman from Waco would
force on him as hate, though Myra sees it as "A terrible, hopeless, twisted
kind of *love*." She proves she is right when she herself turns on him at the
end.

While human, profane love is portrayed as selfish and the momentary
communion between individuals which it may provide as ultimately more
destructive than redemptive, sacred love fares no better. Vee Talbott's sublimation of her sexual frustration seems to be the basis for the sacramental
vision which causes her to see and paint her neighbors as biblical figures.
Her inability to cope with the material world (symbolized by her general
awkwardness and periodic attacks of blindness) leads, finally, to madness.
There is no place in the material, mercantile world for Vee even though she
is partially related to the powerful forces of darkness in her religious intolerance and her ministrations to Jabe. She has been tainted by vision and is
survived by the harpy-like Temple sisters who trade on the gossip-value of
original mystery and touch up the strains of tragedy for use in their own
synthetic religious rites based not on vision but on the description of the
tragic events as rendered in what has become scripture for them, a newspaper
called the *Commercial Appeal*.

Religious and artistic vision are closely related in the play. When we
first meet Val Xavier, he is carrying a dish of sherbet which Vee has made
for Jabe's homecoming. Vee has made herself Val's patroness and by means
of the confection both are imagistically related to Myra's Confectionery, the
artificial bower of bliss and garden of Eden which Myra is to set up behind
the "dry goods" section of the store: the world of vision for the ascetic, of
dream for the artist and of passionate love for the matron are emblematically
realized by the confectionery where sweetness is all. By the end of the play,
however, we see the sweetness turn to bitterness and, from the beginning
of the play, we are made aware that the confectionery is doomed to destruction. The lost paradise of the confectionery is where Myra conceived her
love child by Val, the child which is never born in the play. Val's own
immaculately conceived love child, his book in the composing of which he
hopes to make sense out of existence and which Myra compares to a baby
is likewise destroyed—we never hear of the manuscript again. Artists, not
only Val but a Negro musician, Loon, are considered misfits in the world
the play posits and they are made to leave it.

Though the play with its Easter imagery is concerned with myths of
rebirth and resurrection, the action of *Battle of Angels* ends, significantly, on

Good Friday with the death of the protagonists and not on Easter Sunday. The epilogue, it is true, takes place like the prologue, on Sunday, but what we learn through the action of the play is that death and chaos have taken a heavy toll and that what survives is either ludicrous like the Temple sisters or subject to perennial destruction like the life symbolized in the snakeskin jacket. As Val pointedly remarks to Myra about Jabe's presence in her confectionery: "Death's in the orchard, Myra!" Persephone's world, her orchard of fertility, lost paradise and dream world are all subject to death, the real proprietor of all real estate. Posted at every exit to Jabe's hell are his hounds and throughout the play we hear them baying.

The gods, for Williams, seem to work through the features of men's psyches and the characters in *Battle of Angels* are not entirely innocent of aggravating given horror by their demonic conduct toward one another. Even lovers like Myra and Val are capable of seeing and treating each other as dog and fox. Human possessiveness and selfishness are not excused as fated actions. Myra, jealous of Cassandra's love for Val, would have her tied up like a hound: "When dogs go mad they ought to be locked and chained," she says. Though he may understand it, Williams does not condone Myra's viciousness. The woman from Waco who leads the hounds that pursue Val to the lynching tree is described by Williams as feverish and sinister, a dyed blonde wearing masklike makeup and *"falsely glittering gems on her fingers which are knotted tight around her purse."* She is thus linked with the falseness of appearances and the mercantile forces of society. However, by describing her as a feverish victim of age, frustration and obsession, Williams seems to ask our pity for her as well. Even Jabe, the most vicious character in the play is, to the extent that he is human, made pitiable by the fact that he is dying of cancer. Though Williams may rail against social repression, hypocrisy, intolerance and inequity, unlike playwrights of the social meliorist persuasion (from Brecht to Odets and Miller) or playwrights of the moral didactic type (like Sartre) his primary criticism is not of human ethical behavior but of what he portrays as its tragic, irremediable source, the ill-designed creation which favors, nurtures and prospers death even in the very act of propagating life.

During the catastrophe in the third act of *Battle of Angels*, Cassandra shouts above the turmoil on and off stage: "A battle in heaven. A battle of *angels* above us! And *thunder!* And *storm!*" Her lines are identical with those at the end of a poem which Williams wrote called "The Legend" dealing with the myth of the Fall. When the gates of paradise are closed against Adam and Eve, the angels, according to Williams's adaptation of the myth, are fighting among themselves. The battle of the good and evil angels, he shows in the poem, is continuous though Adam and Eve, aware only of their desire for each other, ignore or do not perceive the great peril of their situation in a cosmos where even the highest creatures are engaged in strife:

> but they, being lost
>   Could not observe an omen—
>   they knew only
> the hot, quick arrow of love
>   while metals clashed,
>   a battle of angels above them,
> and thunder—and storm!

The ominousness of cosmic strife (see, for example, Sebastian Venable's Darwinian garden in *Suddenly Last Summer*) and the persistence of psychological conflict (almost all of Williams's darkest plays reveal the Cerberus beneath the skin of their protagonists) have constituted the basic fabric of Williams's theatrical vision throughout his career. In his introduction to Carson McCullers's *Reflections in a Golden Eye*, Williams attempted an apologia for the artist's concern with violence and horror. He sees the artist as one called to deliver "the message of Absolute Dread" which he defines as "that Sense of the Awful which is the desperate black root of nearly all significant modern art, from the *Guernica* of Picasso to the cartoons of Charles Addams." In the form of a discussion with a hypothetical reader hostile to "these writers [who] have to write about crazy people doing terrible things" Williams explains that characters and their actions are merely "externals" or "symbols" chosen to "concentrate" and "compress" the artist's spiritual intuition of "something almost too incredible and shocking to talk about." *Battle of Angels* is important as an early example of Williams's ambitious attempt to portray what he considers by nature indefinable, a something ("the horror, the horror" perhaps) buried in the very nature of existence.

RUBY COHN

The Garrulous Grotesques of Tennessee Williams

The last plays of Eugene O'Neill were produced after World War II; the first plays of Arthur Miller and Tennessee Williams were produced after World War II. Though Miller and Williams strain, like O'Neill, toward tragedy, each of them early settled into his own idiom, little tempted by O'Neill's restless experimentation. Since Miller and Williams dominated a decade of American theater, their names have often been coupled, if only for contrast. The British critic Kenneth Tynan wrote of them: "Miller's plays are hard, 'patrist,' athletic, concerned mostly with men. Williams's are soft, 'matrist,' sickly, concerned mostly with women. What links them is their love for the bruised individual soul and its life of 'quiet desperation.' " What also links them is the dramaturgy whereby those souls are bruised; not at all quiet in their desperation, these victim-souls indulge in language to evoke our pity. The most effective dialogue of Miller often relies on his Jewish background, whereas that of Williams leans on his southern background.

Always expansive, Williams has written many more plays than Miller, but they do not all deserve close attention. Williams often reuses the same materials—phrase, theme, scene, or character. Williams himself acknowledged: "My longer plays emerge out of earlier one-acters or short stories I may have written years before. I work over them again and again." Consistently, Williams reworks by expansion, and comparison of the short works with the longer plays illuminates his focus on dialogue of pathos.

The Glass Menagerie, Williams's first popular play, emerged in several stages from a fifteen-page short story, written in the early 1940s but not

From *Dialogue in American Drama.* © 1971 by Indiana University Press.

published until 1948. In dramatizing the story, Williams wrote four, perhaps five, versions. A one-act play may have preceded a movie scenario called *The Gentleman Caller*, which was submitted to MGM in 1943. Subsequently, Williams wrote a five-scene, sixty-page play, twenty-one pages of which were incorporated into a seven-scene, hundred-and-five page typescript (now in the University of Virginia library). This last manuscript became the so-called "reading version" of *The Glass Menagerie*, and it is better known than the final eight-scene revision, first staged in 1944.

The original short story, "Portrait of a Girl in Glass," contains four characters—the narrator Tom, his nameless mother, his sister Laura, and a red-headed Irishman named Jim Delaney. The first half of the story is largely expository, but the second half is the kernel of the Gentleman Caller scenes of the dramatic versions. In the story, Laura is not lame, but she has withdrawn so deeply into her private world that she is not quite sane. In the story, Laura and Jim share no high school past, but, because he has freckles, she equates him with the freckled, one-armed orphan in a novel by Gene Stratton Porter—as real to her as her St. Louis apartment. In "Portrait of a Girl in Glass," Laura "covered the walls with shelves of little glass articles," but the articles have no particular shape. As in Williams's subsequent dramas, Tom brings Jim to dinner, but Laura does not show him her glass collection. As in the dramatic versions, Laura and Jim dance after dinner, but they scarcely converse; Laura's entire dialogue is: "Oh—you have freckles! . . . Freckles? . . . What?"

The most sustained dialogue of the short story begins with the interruption of Laura's mother:

> "Good heavens! Laura? Dancing?"
> Her look was absurdly grateful as well as startled.
> "But isn't she stepping all over you, Mr. Delaney?"
> "What if she does?" said Jim, with bearish gallantry. "I'm not made of eggs!"
> "Well, well, well!" said Mother, senselessly beaming.
> "She's light as a feather!" said Jim. "With a little more practice she'd dance as good as Betty!"
> There was a little pause of silence.
> "Betty?" said Mother.
> "The girl I go out with!" said Jim.
> "Oh!" said Mother.
> She set the pitcher of lemonade carefully down and with her back to the caller and her eyes on me, she asked him just how often he and the lucky young lady went out together.

"Steady!" said Jim.

Mother's look, remaining on my face, turned into a glare of fury.

"Tom didn't mention that you went out with a girl!"

"Nope," said Jim. "I didn't mean to let the cat out of the bag. The boys at the warehouse'll kid me to death when Slim gives the news away."

He laughed heartily but his laughter dropped heavily and awkwardly away as even his dull senses were gradually penetrated by the unpleasant sensation the news of Betty had made.

"Are you thinking of getting married?" said Mother.

"First of next month!" he told her.

It took several moments to pull herself together. Then she said in a dismal tone, "How nice! If Tom had only told us we could have asked you *both!*"

The story's climactic revelation is softened in the play—Jim first reveals his engagement to Laura, and then, separately, to Amanda, so that we watch the effect on each of them. Laura is almost wordless as she gives Jim the broken glass unicorn—"A—souvenir." But Amanda nags Tom so vociferously that he leaves the family shortly afterwards. Williams has expanded the story to evoke our compassion for all four characters.

As Williams developed the Gentleman Caller incident from story to short play, and then again to full-length play, he had room to intensify the pathos. Except for a residual "Freckles" in the reading version, Laura no longer identifies Jim with the Gene Stratton Porter character; she no longer reads to escape from reality. No longer "foolish" as in the story, Laura appeals to us by her fragility—lameness, pleurosis, and pathological shyness. Though Amanda refuses to use the word "crippled," Laura faces that reality about herself. She talks to Jim about "clumping up the aisle with everyone watching" even as we have watched her clump around the stage. Because she is lame, the dancing scene is poignant. But Williams also bends her few sentences to evoke our pity, and he emphasizes the glass menagerie—both verbally and theatrically—to show Laura's pathos.

As far back as high school, sensitive Laura was attracted to worldly Jim. Neither a gentleman nor a caller on Laura, the "gentleman caller" mouths clichés of practicality and progress, but his actual career has been a constant retrogression from its high school pinnacle. At the warehouse, Jim evidently uses Tom to recall his high school glory, and in the apartment Jim audibly uses Laura to bolster his sagging self-confidence. Reduced to stale jokes, sports reports, and makeshift psychology, Jim boasts: "I'm not made of glass." (as opposed to the story's less pointed: "I'm not made of eggs!"). However, we can read his fragility through his veneer of psychology, electrodynamics, and public speaking. While dancing with Laura, Jim bumps into a table, breaking the horn of Laura's glass unicorn. As even Jim knows, unicorns are "extinct in the modern world." In the remainder of the scene, Jim virtually breaks Laura, a girl in glass, who lives on imagination and is therefore almost extinct in the modern world. After Jim pays attention to Laura with well-worn clichés—"I'm glad to see that you have a sense of humor." "Did anybody ever tell you that you were pretty?" "I'm talking to you sincerely."—after he kisses her, he reveals that he will not call again because he is engaged to Betty. By the time Amanda intrudes upon the intimacy of Laura and Jim, the brief romance is over. Vulnerable as Jim is in the wider world, he has been injurious to the world of the glass menagerie. The Gentleman Caller of the old South has been replaced by a pathetic shipping clerk of industrial St. Louis, and even he has other allegiances.

More complex than either Jim or Laura, Tom evolves considerably from the narrator of the short story. Designated as a poet in the final version of the play, Tom carries Williams's lyric flights, his verbal creation of atmosphere, and his ironic commentary upon the action. Unlike Wilder's State Manager, Tom remains a character in his own right—fond of his sister, ambiguous about his mother, and eager to follow in his father's escapist footsteps. As Laura is symbolized by her glass unicorn, Tom is symbolized by his movies, which we know only through dialogue. He explains movies to his mother as sublimated adventure, but by the time Jim comes to the house, Tom is tired of vicarious adventures: "People go to the *movies* instead of *moving*. . . . I'm tired of the movies and I'm about to move!" Tom's final speech tells us how far he has moved, and yet he has been unable to escape Proustian recollections of his sister, which are inevitably triggered by colored glass or music.

Though Narrator Tom closes *The Glass Menagerie* on our view of Laura blowing out her candles in a world lit by lightning, the stage viability of the play has always rested upon the character of Amanda. No longer the mere martinet of the short story, she possesses as many qualities "to love and pity . . . as to laugh at." She speaks the most distinctive as well as the most extensive dialogue of the play. It is Amanda who names Laura's collection a "glass menagerie," in which animal drives are frozen into esthetic objects, and it is she who longs for gentleman callers in an ungentle world. At once nostalgic about her genteel past and minimally practical about the sordid present, she punctuates her drawling elegance with sharp questions and terse commands. She recalls every detail of the balls of her youth, and she goes into absurd physiological detail about the daily lives, and especially meals, of her children. In the final version of the play, Williams heightens the Southern quality of her speech, increases her use of "honey" to Laura, her nagging of Tom, and her repetitions. The cumulative effect of these final revisions (particularly the added opening lines about her rejection at church) is to endear her to us, and to evoke pity for the garrulous mother, as for the timid daughter.

After the Gentleman Caller leaves, near the end of the play, Amanda accuses Tom: "You live in a dream; you manufacture illusions!" But the play's pathos arises from the illusions manufactured by *all* the characters. Though the glass menagerie is most directly relevant to Laura, all four characters have sublimated their animal drives into esthetics. Laura has her glass animals, Tom his movies and poems, Amanda her jonquil-filled memories distorted into hopes, and Jim his baritone clichés of progress.

The Glass Menagerie has often been called Chekhovian in its atmospheric rendition of a dying aristocracy. As the last scene opens, a blackout pointedly occurs while Jim and Amanda toast the Old South. What dies into darkness, however, is not a class but a frail feminine household, and we do not feel, as in Chekhov's plays, that the household represents a class. In subsequent plays, however, Williams dramatizes various aspects of the disintegration of the Old South. The cumulative effect embraces a dying civilization, which makes its impact through rhythm and imagery.

Three years separate *The Glass Menagerie* from Williams next extended drama, *A Streetcar Named Desire* (1947). Two one-act plays written during that interval point toward the latter. *Streetcar*, like *The Glass Menagerie*, is a poignant portrait of a southern gentlewoman who is "extinct in the modern world." Similarly, the pathetic protagonists of two 1945 one-acters take refuge from reality in a world of fantasy. Thirteen-year-old Willie in *This Property is Condemned* invents her own romanticized life in imitation of her prostitute sister, Alva, who is dead. Miss Lucretia Collins, a demented old maid in *Portrait of a Madonna*, imagines herself pregnant by a youthful lover; like Blanche Dubois in *Streetcar*, she is taken to an institution by a doctor and nurse. Both Willie and Miss Lucretia are as garrulous as Amanda Wingfield. Lacking her energy, however, they exist only through their brave, bright words, which are contradicted by the sexless pathos of their visual stage reality—child and old maid. But Blanche Dubois is Williams's masterpiece of contradiction.

The very name Blanche Dubois suggests her duality. In the play, she herself translates it for Mitch as "white woods. Like an orchard in spring." But even her translation is a fantasy. Blanche is past her spring, and the purity of Blanche-white is undermined by the thicket of Dubois-woods. Anglicized, Blanche's name is Duboys, and under her chaste surface, Blanche lusts for boys. Comparably, her clothes reflect her divided nature—mothlike white for day and red satin robe for intimacy. More pointedly, the two streetcars—Desire and Cemeteries—suggest the opposing forces that claim Blanche. Her deeds—impulsive and reckless—give the lie to her words— consciously poetic and proper. Blanche never understands the deep division within her, as Williams understands that division in himself: "Roughly there was a combination of Puritan and Cavalier strains in my blood which may be accountable for the conflicting impulses I often represent in the people I write about." The Dubois sisters seem to have only the one Puritan (French Huguenot) strain in *their* blood, but Blanche is nevertheless prey to "conflicting impulses." Preserving the veneer of an aristocratic belle of the Old South, criticizing her sister for an animal marriage, Blanche herself slips into vulgarisms. Though she claims to be "compiling a notebook of quaint little words and phrases" of the New Orleans milieu, she has, as Stanley charges, heard them all before.

Early in the play, Blanche sprays Stanley with her atomizer, so that he responds: "If I didn't know that you was my wife's sister I'd get ideas about you!" Later, Blanche tells Stella that the only way to live with Stanley "is to—go to bed with him." While waiting for Mitch, Blanche toys amorously with a newspaper boy who has just had a cherry soda. "Cherry!" Blanche teases, confessing, "You make my mouth water." Much later that night, Blanche mocks Mitch: *"Voulez-vous coucher avec moi ce soir?"* The question has wider currency than the French language, and Blanche takes a risk for her poor little joke—the risk of destroying her pure southern belle image in the opinion of Mitch. A few minutes later, *"she rolls her eyes"* when she mentions her "old-fashioned ideals" to Mitch. But that is the last time she shows any awareness of playing a role.

During most of the eleven scenes of the play, Blanche appears to believe in her role of proper southern lady, and that way her madness lies. In scene 1, Blanche plays the *grande dame* for her own sister, until her impassioned outburst about death at Belle Reve. In scene 2, she plays a sex kitten for Stanley (which is compatible with the cliché portrait of a vivacious southern lady); as she protects her love letters and delivers the Belle Reve papers to him, she explains that all the male Dubois "exchanged the land for their epic fornications." Only obliquely does she admit that the plantation is finally foreclosed to pay for her own fornications. The very name Belle Reve feminizes dreams since *rêve* is a masculine noun and *belle* a feminine adjective.

In scene 3, Blanche plays the refined lady—her sustained pose with Mitch: "I can't stand a naked light bulb, any more than I can a rude remark or a vulgar action." In scene 4, Blanche plays the outraged aristocrat, complaining of animal Stanley, and culminating in her plea to Stella: "*Don't— don't hang back with the brutes!*" In scene 5, Blanche acts superior to Stanley even when he hints at her past. In scene 6, Blanche continues to play the refined lady for Mitch, but the memory of her marriage tears through that role. She is only momentarily present in scene 7, but her aristocratic role is shattered in scene 8, when Stanley gives her a bus ticket back to Laurel, an ironic name for the town of her humiliation. When Mitch arrives in scene 9, Blanche attempts briefly to resume her refined lady role, then abruptly confesses and explains her promiscuities: "Death . . . The opposite is desire." Rather than suffer the desire of Mitch, however, Blanche cries out wildly: "Fire! Fire! Fire!" In the climactic tenth scene, both Blanche and Stanley have been drinking. We are not quite sure whether her story of Shep Hunt-leigh is an illusion or a brave front against Stanley, who scoffs at her pose of purity. Forcing Blanche to drop the broken bottle-top of self-defense, Stanley calls her "Tiger." Earlier, she had called Stanley an animal, but now the animal accusation is turned against her. In the final scene, Blanche is the victim of her own southern-belle fantasy; the role has become her reality as she seems not to recognize the poker-playing men. Expecting Shep Hunt-leigh, Blanche responds to the Institution doctor, who is both her Hunter and her Shepherd. Her exit line, addressed to the doctor, intensifies her pathos: "Whoever you are—I have always depended on the kindness of strangers." But we know that Blanche has found no kindness among strangers, and we may recall her first use of the word "strangers," in her confession to Mitch: "After the death of Allan—intimacies with strangers was all I seemed able to fill my empty heart with."

To play her role in the two-room Kowalski apartment, Blanche has brought a trunk full of clothes; her stage business involves drinking, dimming lights, emerging from hot baths, and seeking compliments about her appearance. But it is mainly through her dialogue that Blanche underlines her manor-born superiority. She introduces cultural references into the French Quarter dwelling, which evokes an Edgar Allen Poe horror story for her. She recognizes that the lines on Mitch's cigarette case belong to a sonnet by Mrs. Browning; she has evidently taught American literature, since she mentions Poe, Hawthorne, and Whitman. She calls the newspaper boy a young Prince out of the Arabian nights, and Mitch her Rosenkavalier, Armand, and Samson. In the last scene, Blanche is blind to the reality of her situation, but she specifies that her jacket is Della Robbia blue: "the blue of the robe in the old Madonna pictures."

Blanche's speech is distinguished not only by her cultural references. She alone uses correct grammar and varied syntax. Her vocabulary contains such Latinisms as "heterogeneous," "absconding," "judicial," "transitory," and "recriminations." But when Blanche uses images, they are stale or incongruous. Defeated, she tells Mitch that she had viewed him as "a cleft in the rock of the world that I could hide in." A little later, she compares her past to "an old tin can [on] the tail of the kite." Of her soldier boy-friends, Blanche remarks: "The paddy-wagon would gather them up like daisies." Even her most moving speech—the story of her husband's suicide—closes with pretentious imagery: "And then the searchlight which had been turned on the world was turned off again and never for one moment since has there been any light that's stronger than this—kitchen—candle." Seemingly related but not functionally linked is her hope that Stella's baby will have eyes "like two blue candles lighted in a white cake."

When Blanche tries to be uplifting, her images are most inadequate. Seeking to inspire Stella, she becomes trite and abstract: poetry and music, new light, tender feelings, our flag. When Blanche insists upon her superiority to Stanley, she can summon only the cliché phrases of popular magazines: "But beauty of the mind and richness of the spirit and tenderness of the heart—and I have all of those things—aren't taken away, but grow!" Whatever Williams may have intended, Blanche Dubois is trapped by the poverty of her imagery which reflects the poverty of her dreams, like Miller's Willie Loman. But whereas Miller supplies Willy with weak foils, Blanche is challenged and destroyed by a strong antagonist, Stanley Kowalski, whom she correctly views as her executioner.

The hard consonants of Stanley Kowalski contrast with the open vowels of Blanche Dubois. As opposed to her mothlike whiteness, Stanley moves in a world of vivid color; Williams compares him to *"a richly feathered male bird."* Stanley wears a green bowling shirt or bright silk pyjamas. He and Stella make love under colored lights. His poker party resembles Van Gogh's *Night Cafe*, with its *"raw colors of childhood's spectrum."*

Visually and verbally, Williams opposes Stanley to Blanche. Each character is summarized by his opening lines:

> STANLEY: Hey, there! Stella, Baby! . . . Catch! . . . Meat!
> BLANCHE: They told me to take a streetcar named Desire, and
>   then transfer to one called Cemeteries and ride six blocks
>   and get off at—Elysian Fields!

Stanley has trained his wife to catch his meat, in every sense. Blanche has come to the end of the line named Desire, and Williams's drama traces her ride to Cemeteries. Forcing her toward that destination is the implacable solidity of Stanley's speech: "Be comfortable is my motto." "You going to shack up here?" "To hold front position in this rat-race you've got to believe you are lucky." "You left nothing here but spilt talcum and old empty perfume bottles—unless it's the paper lantern you want to take with you."

On stage, Stanley's physicality contrasts with Blanche's ready verbalizations. His cruellest gesture in the play is to tear the paper lantern off the light bulb, in order to hand it to Blanche. His other rough acts are understandable—tossing the meat package to Stella, ruffling Blanche's rich clothes, throwing the radio out of the window, breaking plates when he is insulted, and handing Blanche a one-way ticket to Laurel. We do not see Stanley hit Stella, and we do not see him rape Blanche; the first deed is mitigated by his contrition, and the second by Blanche's provocation. In the last scene of the play, however, when Blanche is helpless and defeated, Stanley acts with the kind of cruelty that Blanche has called "unforgiveable," and of which she herself was guilty when she told her young husband: "You disgust me."

Blanche and Stanley are protagonist and antagonist in *Streetcar*, and yet, whatever Williams has said in commentary, his play is not a simple picture of victim and villain. Blanche is cruel to her husband, rude to Eunice, patronizing to Stella, and arrogant to Stanley. Though Stanley is finally cruel to Blanche, he is a faithful friend to Mitch and a satisfying husband to Stella. Especially as played by Marlon Brando, Stanley hides vulnerability beneath taunts and boasts; his cruelty defends his world.

Between Blanche and Stanley are Stella and Mitch, each part-victim and part-brute. Naturally kind, admittedly sensual, Stella is ironically named for a star. She remembers Belle Reve without nostalgia, and she lives contentedly in the Elysian Fields, acquiescing to Stanley's dominance as quietly as she evidently did to Blanche in their childhood. "Thrilled" by Stanley, she accepts all facets of his violence—except the truth of his rape of her sister.

Like Stella, Mitch is pulled between Stanley and Blanche. Responsive to women, Mitch willingly accedes to Blanche's instructions in gentility, and he suffers visibly at Stanley's revelations about her past. An Army buddy, fellow-worker, and poker pal of Stanley, Mitch shares Stanley's ethics— "Poker should not be played in a house with women." But he also shares Blanche's awareness of death. Mitch has a dead girlfriend as Blanche has a dead husband. As Blanche watched the members of her family die, Mitch is watching his mother die. Mitch's feeling for his dying mother elicits Blanche's confession of her husband's suicide. Death makes them realize their need of one another. But after Mitch learns about Blanche's past, a

Mexican woman chants: "Flores. Flores. Flores para los muertos." It is not clear whether Blanche understands the Spanish, but she reminisces on the same theme: "Death—I used to sit here and she used to sit over there and death was as close as you are." Death of the mind is precisely as close to Blanche as is Mitch. By the next scene, even before the rape, Blanche panics into derangement.

The play's last scene so victimizes Blanche—sister, brother-in-law, poker players, nurse—that it borders on sentimentality, which is aggravated, in reading, by such pretentious stage directions as *"tragic radiance"* for Blanche, on whose face *"all human experience shows."* But Williams saves the scene by the very triviality of the dialogue—Blanche's preoccupation with her adornments, the men's preoccupation with their poker game. Both preoccupations have been repeated during the course of the play, so that they take on cumulative significance in this last scene. Other repeated motifs culminate in this scene—the Shep Huntleigh of Blanche's fantasy, her hot bath and search for compliments, her references to death, the distortion of the "Varsouviana" into jungle noises, Stanley's revelation of the naked light bulb. At the last, Blanche follows the doctor as blindly as she followed Stella during the first poker game. Once Blanche is gone, civilized discourse vanishes, Stanley and Stella relax into an almost wordless animal abandon as we hear the blue piano music and the final words of the play: "This game is seven-card stud," which summarizes life in the French Quarter.

Williams had intended at first to call his play *The Poker Game*, and the actual title may indicate his shift of focus from Stanley to Blanche. Elia Kazan's much-publicized Director's Notes center every scene on Blanche, whose role has been called an "actor-killer." Though the psychopathology of Blanche has absorbed two decades of critics, directors like Kazan build from climax to climax of the play on the firm ground of Stanley's brute vigor. While Blanche's desire goes the way of Belle Reve, Stanley and his entourage raucously ride the streetcar named Desire. Like D. H. Lawrence, Williams presents desire as synonymous with life, and its opposite is Cemeteries. Before the play began, Blanche used desire to escape from death, but in the Elysian Fields, the world of seven-card stud, her past desires turn to present death, and Williams summons our pity with light, music, repetition, and her paste-images that she displays like diamonds.

Though Williams was never to match the shock effect of scene 10 and the pathos of scene 2 of *Streetcar*, he built his subsequent drama on this basic combination of shock and pathos. New on the stage, that mixture is central to the southern grotesque tradition, which finds in deviates a warmth that is absent from normal members of society. Like other members of the southern gothic tradition, Williams strives to establish the mythic importance of his grotesques. To do this, he introduces increasingly obvious symbols into his plays.

In 1948, Williams wrote two plays that show the determination of his symbolism (and a concomitant weakness of his dialogue)—*Ten Blocks on the Camino Real* and *Summer and Smoke*. The first of these was revised and expanded in 1953. Though the second was also revised to *The Eccentricities of a Nightingale*, it is usually played in the first version. The source of both plays is Williams's short story, "The Yellow Bird." In that story, a minister's daughter, Alma, rebels against her background. Following in the footsteps of an ancestor who was burned as a witch when she obeyed the injunctions of a yellow bird named Bobo, the twentieth century Alma progresses from smoking to dying her hair, to "juking" with men. Happily ensconced in the old French Quarter of New Orleans, she bears an illegitimate child who presents her with "fists full of gold and jewels that smelled of the sea." When the child grows up, he goes off to sea, and when Alma dies, she is reclaimed by the child's father, who appears like Neptune with a cornucopia. Alma's son erects a monument to her memory—"three figures of indeterminate gender astride a leaping dolphin," whose name is Bobo, like the provocative yellow bird of Alma's ancestor.

Summer and Smoke seems to have imploded from this fanciful celebration of sexual freedom. Pushed back to the early years of the twentieth century, Alma's sexual rigidity recalls that of Emma in O'Neill's *Diff'rent;* in both plays, the sexually inhibited woman turns to perverse behavior. But Williams is even more lavish with the dialogue of his southern characters than is O'Neill with his not so laconic New Englanders. And though O'Neill's play is schematic in its condemnation of the Puritannical "difference," it is less simplistic than that of Williams, which is a long *carpe diem*. Under the stone angel of Eternity, mere flesh should gather rosebuds while and where it may. Dr. John Buchanan gathers a literal Rosa Gonzales, when Alma provides nothing but soul. For several scenes, John and Alma engage in a virtual medieval debate between body and soul. After John's father dies, however, and he is offered a combination of attractive body and soul in Nellie Ewell, Alma and John change sides in the debate. "The tables have turned with a vengeance!" By the end of the play, John's wild oats sowed, he snuggles up to wife and career, while Alma sets about seducing a young traveling salesman, who will be the first of a series.

Containing more discussion than Williams's previous plays, *Summer and*

Smoke also strives to shock through violence—John throws a wild party, John's father strikes Rosa's father, Rosa's father shoots John's father—but the violence is peripheral and *recherché,* since the eruptions do not arise out of the situations. Violence and discussion seem to belong in different plays. As characters, sexy John and soulful Alma often disappear into their debates. They are even less substantial than the titular Summer and Smoke, which imply the concreteness of heat and fire.

Conversely, Williams's *The Rose Tattoo* (1950) suffers from too much concreteness, with obvious symbolic intention. Again the theme is *carpe diem,* but instead of gathering rosebuds, Williams gushes roses. The dead but ever-virile husband of the protagonist is named Rosario Delle Rose, his daughter Rosa Delle Rose. The Delle Rose home has rose-patterned wallpaper and rose-colored carpet. When first seen, protagonist Serafina wears a pale rose silk dress and a rose in her hair. Her husband's mistress has ordered him a rose silk shirt, and she lays a bunch of roses on his grave. Rosario Delle Rose had a rose tattooed on his chest, and that rose appeared on his wife's breast after she conceived. Only slightly less blatant, are the dialogue references to roses. Three years after the death of Rosario Delle Rose, his wife Serafina recalls her husband as "a rose of a man," and declares: "The memory of the rose in my heart is perfect!" But her would-be lover tries to dim that memory by applying rose oil in his own hair and having a rose tattooed on his own chest. After a night with her new lover, Serafina declares: "Just now I felt on my breast the burning again of the rose." By such hammering, Williams pounds the fertility symbol to the edge of farce. He probably intended *The Rose Tattoo* to be something of a saturnalia, a joyous celebration of sex, but (when we are not simply bored) we tend to laugh *at* rather than *with* the celebrants.

The dialogue of the play, like its roses, strains for celebration. Larded with Italian phrases and locutions, the English is surprisingly grammatical, the vocabulary extensive, and the emotions self-consciously expressed. As in *Summer and Smoke,* violence erupts almost gratuitously—Rosa tries to cut her wrists, a traveling salesman digs his knee into Alvaro's groin, Alvaro captures a rampaging goat, then pursues Serafina around the room. Williams specifies: *"The chase is grotesquely violent and comic."* But it is superfluous. As are Williams's directions that the final scene *"should be played with the panto-mimic lightness, almost fantasy, of early Chaplin comedy."* This is abandoning dialogue for mime, but even in this domain Williams insists upon a symbolism of which Chaplin is rarely guilty. In the last scene, a hill full of women flourish the rose-colored shirt like a banner. Accompanied by music, the flag of sex *"moves in a zig-zag course through the pampas grass to the very top of the embankment, like a streak of flame shooting up a dry hill."* And after the flag runs Serafina, whose name promises fine nights.

Five years later, in *Cat on a Hot Tin Roof* (1955), Williams creates Maggie the Cat, who longs to offer such fine nights. In *The Rose Tattoo*, the Delle Rose cottage is topped by a tin roof, which sizzles in the Gulf Coast summer. In *Ten Blocks on the Camino Real* (1948), a hotel proprietor remarks: "The girls in the Panama clip-joints are drinking Blue Moons, the gobs and the sea-going bell-hops are getting stewed, screwed and tattooed, and the S.P.'s are busy as cats on a hot tin-roof!" Some time between 1952, when Williams published "Three Players of a Summer Game" and 1955, when *Cat on a Hot Tin Roof* was first produced, Williams came to associate Margaret Pollitt with that metaphor of monosyllables—cat on a hot tin roof.

Of the "three players of a summer game," none is Margaret Pollitt. In the story she is never compared to a cat, and she is never called Maggie. But Brick Pollitt, her husband, is transplanted almost intact from story to play. In both story and play, Brick takes to drink for sexual reasons, but in the story it is Margaret's parasitic masculinity that is responsible. "Margaret Pollitt lost her pale, feminine prettiness and assumed in its place something more impressive—a firm and rough-textured sort of handsomeness." Margaret thrives on Brick's weakness, but a widow and her daughter play croquet with Brick, seeking to restore his self-respect. When the summer is over, widow and daughter leave town, and Brick returns to liquor and wife, who drives him in their Pierce-Arrow "as Caesar or Alexander the Great or Hannibal might have led in chains through a capital city the prince of a state newly conquered."

In *Cat on a Hot Tin Roof*, Williams reverses Brick's passion for his wife to hers for him, and he changes Margaret's masculinity to Brick's fear of his own homosexuality. The story's widow and daughter disappear, to be replaced by Big Daddy, Big Momma, and Gooper Pollitt's brood. But the most important change is reflected in the new title: "Three Players of a Summer Game" suggests the ephemeral nature of their activity, whereas *Cat on a Hot Tin Roof* couples animal and metal, two durables in uncomfortable contact.

The prevalence of animal imagery in *Cat* has been noted by Bernard Dukore: the Negro servants pronounce the family name as "Polly;" Big Daddy eats like a horse; Big Momma charges like a rhino; Mae and Gooper jaw, jabber, and watch like hawks; their children are compared to county fair animals, monkeys, pigs, and no-neck monsters; the celebrants of Big Daddy's birthday sound "like a great aviary of chattering birds," and they are all deep in "catty talk." For no specified reason, Margaret has been nicknamed Maggie the Cat, and she makes three references to herself as a cat on a hot tin roof (in the original version). In reviewing her affair with Skipper, Maggie calls herself a mouse and says she "shot cock-robbin" Skipper. Brick alone is free of animal resonance, and Maggie even calls him "godlike." Only in his confession to Big Daddy does Brick liken his marriage to "two cats on a fence humping." But he refers to the past, before he sought refuge in alcohol.

Like the roses in *The Rose Tattoo* and desire in *Streetcar*, animality in *Cat* is synonymous with life. Grasping, screeching, devouring, the Pollitts are greedily alive, and the shadow of cancer on Big Daddy has made them all the more aggressive in their vigor. The Reverend Tooker announces sententiously that "the Stork and the Reaper are running neck and neck." In *Cat on a Hot Tin Roof*, Mae Pollitt is pregnant while Big Daddy is dying of cancer. By the end of the play Maggie Pollitt lies that she is pregnant while Brick Pollitt may die of alcoholism. Fear of dying and zest for living distinguish the dialogue of *Cat*, and they dramatize Brick rather than Big Daddy as the moribund stranger in this vital family.

Like O'Neill's drinkers, Brick holds his liquor well. So courteous is he that it is difficult to believe that Big Momma and Big Daddy are his parents; so aloof, it is difficult to view acquisitive Gooper as his brother; so cool, it is difficult to imagine him with desire for either woman or man. The darling of father, mother, and wife, Brick repeats the word "disgust" almost as a leitmotif. When Maggie admires Big Daddy because he "drops his eyes to my boobs an' licks his old chops," Brick comments: "That kind of talk is disgusting." In the crucial scene between Brick and his father, Big Daddy asks: "Why do you drink? Why are you throwing your life away, boy, like somethin' disgusting you picked up on the street?" As if taking the word for a cue, Brick answers the question in one word: "DISGUST!" When Brick realizes that Big Daddy is not horrified that he and Skipper might have been lovers, he exclaims: "Don't you know how people *feel* about things like that? How, how *disgusted* they are by things like that?" The word "disgust" is repeated six times before Brick shifts to mendacity as his reason for drinking. Rejecting this excuse, Big Daddy concludes a long speech to Brick: "*I've* lived with mendacity!—Why can't *you* live with it? Hell, you *got* to live with it, there's nothing *else* to *live* with except mendacity, is there?" Though the words appear abstract out of context, they are a coda to the specific lies of

Big Daddy's life, and the italicized words give rhythm and meaning to the coda, which declares that lies are life.

Cat on a Hot Tin Roof thrives on the life of its lies and animality, to all of which Brick reacts with the tall drinks of his disgust. Ironically, his liveliest reaction emerges from his disgust, and it serves death. When Big Daddy accuses Brick of drinking to kill his disgust with his own lie, Brick bares the truth of mortality to his father: *"How about these birthday congratulations, these many, many happy returns of the day, when ev'rybody but you knows there won't be any!"* At the end of the second act, Brick and Daddy enunciate the theme of the play, each in his own idiom:

> BRICK: Mendacity is a system that we live in.
> BIG DADDY: Yes, all liars, all liars, all lying dying liars! . . .
>   Lying! Dying! Liars!

The original version of the play stresses the contrast between Big Daddy's acceptance and Brick's rejection of the lies that are life. Big Daddy proclaims a sexual aversion to Big Momma, as Brick does to Maggie. As Brick voices his disgust, Big Daddy voices *his* disgust. But Brick will not touch his wife, and Big Daddy *"laid* [his]!—regular as a piston" and fathered his two sons. In the act 2 birthday celebration, Big Momma tells Big Daddy: "I even loved your hate and your hardness, Big Daddy!" He muses: *"Wouldn't it be funny if that was true* . . . " In the original ending of the play, after Maggie has lied that she is pregnant, after she has locked Brick's liquor away, she turns out the lights and declares her love for Brick, who responds: "Wouldn't it be funny if that was true?" to close the play.

Williams supplied an alternate ending for *Cat*, at the suggestion of Broadway director Elia Kazan, who wanted (1) Big Daddy to reappear, (2) Brick to change, and (3) Maggie to be more sympathetic. The five new pages introduce slack into the already slack third act. Brick's declaration of life to Gooper, and of admiration to Maggie, is no more convincing than mere declaration ever is. And Maggie becomes more garrulous rather than more sympathetic. In the original version, the last scene highlights the ambiguous relationship of truth and lies; living is lying, but if one continues to live, even that lie can become truth. In that context, Brick's curtain line is a meaningful echo of Big Daddy: "Wouldn't it be funny if that was true?" In the Kazan-inspired ending, however, Williams confusingly introduces the titular metaphor. Maggie tritely links her love with Brick's life, then closes the play with the line: "I'm determined to do it—and nothing's more determined than a cat on a tin roof—is there? Is there, Baby?" The comparison is preposterous, for the whole play has equated the metaphor with nervousness and discomfort, not determination. On the other hand, if Williams *intends* the metaphor to be preposterous in order to win sympathy for Maggie's determination in the face of impossible odds, then Brick cannot acquiesce tacitly, undergoing the change that Kazan requested. In either case, repetition of the metaphor emphasizes the more flaccid writing of the alternate version.

In both *Streetcar* and *Cat*, the life of the dialogue lies in animal vigor. But *Streetcar* is more dramatic because of the tension between a genteel dream and that vigor, whereas catty energy easily overwhelms aloofness in *Cat*. Kazan's directorial instinct did not err in clinging to Big Daddy, who, without pretentiousness, looms like a god of life from his first word "Crap" to his final furious cry. His speech embraces all the living kingdoms: "The human machine is not so different from the animal machine or the fish machine or the bird machine or the reptile machine or the insect machine!" For all the repetitions of the word "machine," they are organic to him. He is tolerant of all forms of sexuality except what is sold. Big Daddy is the richest planter in the Delta—the man whose life and livelihood are organically interrelated. And this man reacts to the news of his death with rage. It is for Big Daddy that Williams precedes his play by the Dylan Thomas line: "Rage, rage against the dying of the light."

Like many colorful characters, Big Daddy manhandles his creator, growing too big for his play. Thus, his reminiscences about Europe, his generalizations about mendacity, and his elephantine joke diffuse the dramatic drive. Unlike Maggie, he never becomes maudlin. In spite of Big Daddy's digressions and Maggie's unfeline sentimentality, however, *Cat* contains concrete and cohesive dramatic dialogue. All Williams's subsequent plays, like most of his previous ones, are marred by pretentious symbols that seek to inflate psychopathology into poetic myth.

ROBERT BECHTOLD HEILMAN

The Middle Years

CAT ON A HOT TIN ROOF

Cat on a Hot Tin Roof (1955) carries on, after eight years, from *Streetcar,* and in some ways also from the slightly later *Summer and Smoke.* In Brick Pollitt there is the inner split that is central in the earlier protagonists, but it is far more intense than those of Alma and John in *Summer and Smoke.* Brick is the product of the same kind of unrelenting imagination of inner discord that created Blanche DuBois. Indeed, his case history has some remarkable resemblances to hers: glamorous youth, the critical trauma that again involves homosexuality and the rejection of a homosexual, alcoholism, disintegration (with the possible loss of the great plantation as an accompanying symptom of decline), all this in a charismatic personality in which charm is the element that longest resists decay. This degree of likeness in key characters helps outline the differences in the plays taken as wholes. Whereas in *Streetcar* hope lies in Stanley and Stella, with their hearty sexuality and insouciant energy, in *Cat* Williams all but demolishes the fertility myth: Gooper and Mae, with their six children, are made vulgar and grasping plotters, realistic versions of the quasi-human worldliness that is done expressionistically in Goldberg and McCann in Harold Pinter's *The Birthday Party* (1958). Such hope as there may be attaches to the title character, Margaret or Maggie, who, in her desperate struggle to save her husband Brick both for herself and for the plantation, and the plantation for them, might be merely a slick popular heroine. She is much more than that: she is, among

From *The Iceman, the Arsonist, and the Troubled Agent: Tragedy and Melodrama on the Modern Stage.* © 1973 by the University of Washington Press.

other things, an embodiment of the Shavian life force, and that means that she is not so plain and simple as she manages to look. She had some complicity in her husband's downfall, since, in a calculated risk, she had broken up his ambiguous relationship with his best friend, Skipper; her devotion to Brick and the plantation is clearly interwoven with her passionate desire not to be poor again, her cool quest of advantage, and her detestation of Gooper and Mae; she can match them in laying strategic traps for the favors of Brick's parents, and in all the ruthless family in-fighting. So she is a person, not a cinematic madonna to the rescue. Still, insofar as the play is hers, it is concerned with a battle against outer forces by a character of what we have called pragmatic wholeness; win or lose, she herself is not looked at tragically, for, though she has some keen perceptions about herself—"[I've] become—*hard! Frantic!—cruel!!*" . . . "I'm not good," and "I destroyed [Skipper]"—her fight is not to discover herself or order herself but to escape from being a victim.

In terms of her vigor, of the frenzy of her struggle, and of the magnitude of her role, the play is Maggie's; after all, she is "the Cat." Yet Williams is pulled in two different directions, one toward the portrait of the strong competitive woman (the line that descends from Lady Macbeth through Ibsen's Rebecca West), the other toward inner conflict that has tragic potential. On the one hand there is all the tension that derives from Maggie's gladiatorial finesse and daring and her thrusts in various directions; on the other hand, there are the larger-looming problems of character that lie in Brick and in his powerful father, Big Daddy, whose presence alone marks a big jump ahead from *Streetcar*. The protracted confrontation of father and son takes up most of the long act 2, almost half the play in its original form. Bound by affection, they offer a sharp contrast: the mild, quasi-clearheaded pseudo serenity of the son, steadily drinking toward the inner "click" that signifies "peace"; and the violent boisterousness of the older man, ironically euphoric in the illusion of a reprieve from cancer (a faint reminiscence of Oedipus' certitude that he has defeated the malign oracle), triumphant, planning new triumphs, among them straightening out Brick.

Yet there is another bond: the old man's cancer, which will kill him, is paralleled by the thing in Brick's mind that Margaret literally calls "malignant." (Symbols flow from Williams: trying drunkenly to repeat a youthful exploit, Brick gets a fractured foot that is analogous to the broken spirit partly due to the ending of football glories: he uses a literal crutch that also defines the role of alcohol for him.) A less tangible, but dramatically more important, bond is a concern for "truth," or, perhaps better, an incomplete invulnerability before it when the other uses it, therapeutically or punitively, as a flail. In the drama of self-knowledge, where tragedy has its roots, Williams appears to be again of different minds. Up to a point Brick does not muffle his sense of fact: he can say, "I'm alcoholic," he acknowledges, "I want to dodge away from [life]," and he defines, "A drinking man's someone who wants to forget he isn't still young an' believing." Though these recognitions seem to go far, they do not "hurt," and that they do not is part of the dramatic evidence that there are still deeper levels of truth to be known.

The gradual revelation of these deeper levels, with an increase of pain that suggests a saving remnant of sentience in Brick, makes extremely effective drama. What is revealed cannot be defined simply; in a long interpolated note Williams inveighs against " 'pat' conclusions, facile definitions" and rightly insists, "Some mystery should be left in the revelation of character." Brick is tensely and even explosively resentful of the view, partly held by Maggie and, it appears, by Gooper and Mae, that his relationship with Skipper was homosexual; he calls it "friendship," his experience of the "one great good true thing in [a man's] life," and he passionately elaborates his notion to Big Daddy. He resents, too, Maggie's view that he and Skipper carried their college relationship on into professional football "because we were scared to grow up," were hanging on to adolescent dreams of glory. We can argue how much of the total truth is represented by each of these views; what is clear is that, however we assess the mixture of ingredients, Brick was inhabiting an idyllic Eden at whose breakup he began his determined push into a surrogate realm of alcoholic peace. Maggie surely has authority when she comments, "life has got to be allowed to continue even after the *dream* of life is—all—over."

As the history is slowly set forth, Brick claims for himself the virtue of honesty; yet his stance is on the whole the pre-tragic one of defensiveness and blame—blame of a mendacious world and particularly of Maggie: he punishes her by refusing to have sexual intercourse with her. She had destroyed the idyll by putting it into Skipper's head that his feeling for Brick was homosexual and thus destroying him. But at this moment Big Daddy, skeptical, puts on the pressure and elicits the fact that, when Skipper had phoned Brick to make a "drunken confession," Brick had hung up. Big Daddy charges, "we have tracked down the lie with which you're disgusted. . . . This disgust with mendacity is disgust with yourself. *You!*—dug the grave of your friend and kicked him in it!—before you'd face truth with him!" It is at this point that we sense the "two minds" in Williams. Big Daddy presses for the ultimate recognition of truth, and his great strength and passion apparently establish this value beyond question. Then Big Daddy himself is challenged a little later when Brick retaliates by letting it slip out to him that he has not escaped cancer, as he supposes; on the contrary, he is really dying of it. But the truth that Big Daddy has to face is that of physical fact, not moral act. Brick, confronted with the latter, cries, "Who *can* face truth? Can *you?*" And insofar as Williams doubts the human ability to face truth, he is of the same mind as O'Neill in the anti-tragic *Iceman*, where an anesthetic Lethe of alcohol is all that makes existence endurable. It is the reversal of George Eliot's requirement, "No opium." Eliot may have had an illusion of strength, but she could imagine the tragic situation rooted in power to endure. In Brick what we find, on the contrary, is the disaster rooted in weakness. He reflects that sense of human incapacity to endure that has appeared in a good deal of modern "serious drama." Dr. Faustus was the man who tried to be God; Miller's Quentin would castigate himself for entertaining the illusion of divine power; but Brick simply found himself accepted as a "god-like being" and then went to pieces when one worshiper challenged another's purity.

Again, however, Williams has an impulse to go beyond the disaster of personality. He is not willing to let Brick be simply a victim, a good man destroyed by the actions of others. For what Big Daddy, acting as prosecutor, establishes is that Brick "dug the grave of [his] friend and kicked him in it" and that that is the source of his malaise. If this does not impute to Brick the hubris of the "overreacher," it at least makes him a man who does evil instead of one who simply suffers evil. We need now to see whether the play continues to regard him as a man of action or simply settles for his passivity and disintegration. It is here that Margaret's efforts to stir him into a resumption of sexual intercourse—including her final theatrical public claim that she is pregnant—take on great dramatic significance. For his rejection of sex is not only a symptom of illness, of one kind or another, but also, as we have seen, a punishment of her; and punishing her is his means of declaring that the guilt is hers, and of keeping his eyes off his own guilt. It is the old story from *Lear* to O'Neill's *Iceman*, of the man living in a melodrama of blame and resisting the tragic self-confrontation. To resume intercourse would be to declare Margaret innocent of his charges against her, or to forgive her, and thus to make possible his acknowledgment and un-derstanding of his own role—in Skipper's death and in his and Margaret's subsequent misery. Williams has imagined an active tragic role for him. The problem is whether Brick can advance beyond the relative comfort of the melodrama he has created for himself, and beyond that, whether Williams is able to conceive of him as transcending the rather familiar role of the sad young man going under.

Again it appears that Williams is of two minds or at least that he was capable of being of two minds. For he wrote two versions of act 3, his own original draft and then, at the urging of his director Elia Kazan, a second one which was used in the first stage production. While both versions end with at least a touch of the-lady-or-the-tiger ambiguity, the first gives little ground for supposing that Margaret can win her battle against Brick's punitive and even self-righteous detachment. In the second version Brick is a little less laconic, gives a touch of support to Margaret's game of publicly claiming pregnancy, and views with admiration her final tactic of throwing out every bottle of the whiskey that he relies on. There is a little more reason to think that he may take the critical step and break out of his own rigidity. Though even here Margaret retains the line, "Oh, you weak, beautiful people who give up . . . ," still she is now permitted a stronger assertion of her own will to rehabilitate him. However, Williams has more of his heart in the first version: a subtly more urgent dialogue conveys this, and besides, Williams is explicit in his prose comment. He cannot, he says, believe that "a conversation, however revelatory," even a "virtual vivisection," can effect much change in "a person in Brick's state of spiritual disrepair."

In rejecting the dramatic convention that a moment of revelation, even a brutally fierce one, can be the equivalent of a conversion, Williams is perhaps unconsciously seeking ground for sticking to the disaster of personality—the history, not of the person of hubris and of eventual insight, but of the person who cannot cope and cannot face the record. Yet in speaking of Brick's decline, Williams twice applies to it the word *tragedy*, another evidence of his persistent attraction to the form. In *Cat*, surely, he reveals a further tendency to get away from, or at least to modify, the pathetic story of collapse. His central character is the man who himself committed the originating deed and who is on the edge of acknowledging his own guilt. Williams catches Brick at a less irremediable stage of collapse than he does Blanche in *Streetcar*, he almost eliminates the element of the victim that is a bona fide part of Blanche, he gives more authority to the protagonist's crucial rejection of another (Blanche's injury to her husband we see in her own memory only after she has become an undependable witness). And in Big Daddy and Margaret there is a spontaneous emphasis on discovering the truth that is hardly present at all in *Streetcar*. Both of them are also potential tragic characters.

SWEET BIRD OF YOUTH

Four years later, in *Sweet Bird of Youth* (1959), Williams, consciously or not, makes Chance Wayne a variation on Brick Pollitt—the charming young man who achieves a premature glory and then, when it fades, himself fades into dope, drink, ruthlessness that is a pointless by-product of ego-saving, low-grade racketeering, immature exhibitionism, cinematic dreams, scheming, and fakery. Chance has had, also, a fund of energy and unscrupulousness that would make him much closer to the traditional hero than Brick was. Yet he has been successful only as a stud, so that in his failure he can be figuratively described, in the stage direction, as "faced with castration." Suddenly in his final half-dozen speeches this character starts speaking of himself with wisdom: he is "nothing," by the "level-of-rot" measure he is "ancient." "I lived on something that time. . . . Gnaws away." Here, with the active man's self-knowledge, Williams pushes on into the technically tragic in a way that he only tentatively approached in *Cat*. Interestingly, he uses a stage direction to insist that "Chance's attitude should be self-recognition but *not* self-pity—a sort of deathbed dignity and honesty apparent in it." Perhaps the use of the insistent stage direction is a symptom of Williams's own subconscious disbelief in this degree of illumination in Chance. There are several problems here. The most important is that Chance has appeared both so shallow and so preposterous that the self-recognition is hardly plausible in terms of character. Williams felt that Brick, in *Cat*, had disintegrated so far that signs of recovery were inadmissible; though Chance is not alcoholic, he suffers from a multifaceted degeneration, including loss of a kind of dignity and single-mindedness that Brick still held on to, that would much more effectually bar a moral pullback. The ending, then, falls into the sentimental.

The sentimental effect is enhanced by another aspect of the method: Williams makes Chance almost an allegorical figure of youth or of the loss of youth (the epigraph is Hart Crane's "Relentless caper for all those who step / The legend of their youth into the noon"), a subject on which characters arbitrarily make many expository remarks. Adult readers are likely to regard the A. E. Housman elegy as the fitting tune for the departure of youth, and to resist the view that the passage of time is tragic, or is a palliative of the falsenesses by which Chance has become a "monster" (the term that his traveling companion, a decayed actress but less muddleheaded person, applies to both Chance and herself; she is a Blanche DuBois who has caught herself just as she is going down the drain). Hence it is exceptionally difficult for brief speeches plus lengthy stage directions to confer dramatic or moral validity on the loss-of-youth theme. At best pushing this theme is a poor substitute for tragic self-confrontation, which is the expectable consequence of Chance's treatment of his girl (he has not killed her, as Othello did Desdemona, but reduced her to a kind of death-in-life). Then at the very end Williams has Chance, not judging himself, but coming forward and, like the Doctor in the morality play, addressing the audience: "I don't ask for your pity, but just for your understanding—not even that—no. Just for your recognition of me in you, and the enemy, time, in us all." At best such a lecture is untragic. But here it is doubly unfortunate because it bluntly demands what it has to earn imaginatively: identification. And in doing so it invites all men to think, not of the quality of man, but of an "enemy"— to assume, that is, the traditional melodramatic stance that justifies an enlarged blind spot for the self. There are, of course, real enemies to be faced, but to include time in that category hardly escapes the bathetic.

MELODRAMAS OF DISASTER

Except in comedies, such as *Period of Adjustment* (1960) and *The Night of the Iguana* (1961), Williams has not again approached characters in terms of crisis, enlightenment, and possible reordering. In both *Orpheus Descending* (1957; a reworking of *Battle of Angels*, 1940) and *Suddenly Last Summer* (1958) he images the destroying of men by horrors and furies, whether these are hardly interpretable irrationalities, or intelligible as symbols of the darker side of a man or of men. *Orpheus* takes as its theme the community's savage ways of excommunicating or destroying "outsider" types, whether natives or visitors, those who inherit something of the "wild" that is not yet "sick with neon." Two of these are women who, like Blanche DuBois, are scarred by past injuries but, unlike her, survive to fight back and meditate or practice different revenges against the cruel and malicious local society. It is this society that is identified with the nether world, with Death and Demons; and the Eurydice character, Lady Torrance, believes that she is returning from it to "life" when she finds herself pregnant by the Orpheus character, Val Xavier, a strolling guitar player. Carol Cutrere flaunts outrageous conduct to let the town "know I'm alive," and the sheriff's wife, putting her "visions" (whether imaginary or willed or hysterical) on canvas, gains a reputation as a "primitive" painter. The cast is one of Williams's largest, and the situation has numerous ramifications; in the medley of conflicts we see evil almost entirely as an outer threat to the major characters, and almost never as the genesis and material of self-understanding. But a certain melodramatic brilliance hangs over the portrayal of hostilities and revenges.

Again in *Suddenly Last Summer* (paired with *Something Unspoken* under the general title of *Garden District;* the common element is a tyrannical woman operating in a context of New Orleans "Garden District" values) Williams presents the outer destructive force, and the weaker beings who are its actual or potential victims or who have a built-in readiness for destruction. Mrs. Venable, a powerful old woman who can push poor relatives around, centered her life in a relationship with her son Sebastian, still a virgin at forty, whose poetic gift she believed she had always protected, whose eccentricities she humored, and whose false steps she corrected. We see her recalling all this after his death, as she is trying to destroy, or at least by surgery render innocuous, Sebastian's cousin Catharine (by promises of support for research Mrs. Venable is trying to bribe a young experimental neurosurgeon to do a lobotomy on Catharine). Catharine was traveling with Sebastian at the time of his death, she had been "disturbed" in the past, at the time of the play she is on a family visit from a sanitarium, and her state of mind is in part connected with her memories of Sebastian's death. Mrs. Venable, who is murderously jealous of Catharine ("He was mine!"), wants to suppress Catharine's "hideous story" of Sebastian's death: he was killed by a mob of naked, starving Spanish children and partly eaten. On the face of it there is the "oedipal situation": Catharine says, "I failed him" (just as Blanche DuBois said, "I'd failed him in some mysterious way"), and reports that "something had broken, that string of pearls that old mothers hold their sons by like a— sort of a—sort of—*umbilical* cord" (one recalls the title of Sidney Howard's play produced in 1926, *The Silver Cord*).

Yet Williams may be doing something more than replaying, even with his own ingenious variations, a familiar tune. For he has left the story ambiguous, and it is not clear whether the oedipal relationship is primary or secondary; it is by no means evident that Mrs. Venable is wrong when she avers that she "held him back from . . . *Destruction!*" Sebastian's impulse to find destruction may be an expression of his filial situation, a projective multiplication of his mother into inescapable harpies in the cosmos; or it may be anterior to all else, a thing in itself which draws his mother, repellently willful as she is, into a role not so simple as it appears—that is, a hypnotic energizing of him without which he might not have survived to forty. Beneath a fine front suitable to "Renaissance princes," as Mrs. Venable puts it, Sebastian has shown some odd interests and almost clinical weaknesses. At the end he manages to invite, to contrive as it were, a death resembling a scene of destruction that he had witnessed years before and had been strangely fascinated by—that is, the destruction of newborn sea turtles by carnivorous birds on the "blazing sand-beach" of a Galapagos island (the Spanish children who destroy him are regularly described in bird images). Besides, there are all sorts of symbolic echoes and parallels: of St. Sebastian, St. Catherine of Ricci (Catharine's "vision"), the search for God, the jungle (with psychological and social implications).

But all the cornucopia of actual and suggestive materials is gradually subdued to one final effect: the climactic revelation of the mode of Sebastian's death. With skillful theatricality Williams produces a shock of horror; then an abrupt curtain. The principal character, so to speak, was dead before the play started, and even alive did not have a consciousness through which we come to understanding; he is another of the somehow inadequate beings who, like Brick Pollitt, seem fated only to slide down, or even subtly construct, a chute into the waste barrels. Mrs. Venable remains a "whole" woman: all energies lavished on aggressively defending a position which she neither questions nor regards as questionable. Catharine continues the frail line of descent from Laura Wingfield through Blanche DuBois (and in some ways even the "fugitive kind," Carol Cutrere): sweetness, shock, illness. From the pathos of victims, the grotesque horror of events, and the hardly modified fierceness of the competitor, Williams makes almost no move toward the tragic form. But he reveals considerable skill in the melodrama of shock.

The Night of the Iguana is focused on one more in the steady line of Williams characters who have had a rapid slide downhill and who lead a touch-and-go existence on the border line between hospitalization and a very shaky survival outside. The Reverend Lawrence Shannon, forced out of the pulpit by misconduct and a "breakdown" (as often in Williams, we hardly know which is prior), now barely manages to hang on either to his job as conductor of vacation bus tours or to his mental health. Ile is another sick man with an early trauma, this one related to punishments for masturbation; among other symptoms, he has a vengefulness which, somewhat like that of Spandrell in Aldous Huxley's *Point Counter Point*, leads him to seduce, or accept seduction by, teenage girls and then punish them by verbal and even physical blows. In the course of the action he does some rather sturdy self-inspection, noting among other things that in seducing women on his bus tours he always first "ravages" them by "pointing out" the "horrors" of the tropical land they are in; and at the end he apparently finds a solution appropriate to comedy, that is to say, a workable arrangement in the world: joining forces with a lusty widowed innkeeper to run a hostelry in which, as hosts, they will each make special contributions to the entertainment of guests of the opposite sex. (Thus his errant sexual prowess will be rendered socially beneficent by institutionalization.) But even this retrieval of quasi strength out of weakness, or of a modus vivendi out of maladjustment to life, depends upon the therapeutic ministrations of Hannah Jelkes, a fortyish virgin who travels around the world with a ninety-seven-year-old grandfather. She supports them, under exhaustingly difficult conditions, as they go, but she has still energy and generosity and understanding enough to establish with Shannon a "communication" that has restorative value for him. Out of "Maggie the Cat," for whom trying to save Brick Pollitt is hardly distinguishable from saving herself, Williams has distilled a special being who approaches secular sainthood.

THE THEME OF SALVATION

The savior or nurse figure is a relatively late arrival in Williams's characterology, and it underwent several metamorphoses between *Period of Adjustment* (1960) and *The Milk Train Doesn't Stop Here Anymore* (1953). In *Period of Adjustment* there is a literal nurse who marries another of Williams's ail-and-retreat figures, this one afflicted with a disabling psychosomatic palsy. She not only takes on the assignment but cosmicizes her role: "The whole world's a big hospital, a big neurological ward and I am a student nurse in it" (almost at the end). Her words summarize a good deal of the Williams world—a world of human disasters unless someone comes to the rescue.

Hannah Jelkes in *The Night of the Iguana* is a more sophisticated, though still romantic, version of the nurse. But the savior or helper figure becomes most interesting in *The Milk Train Doesn't Stop Here Anymore*, in which Williams employs much more indirection and ambiguity. The savior cannot save, in any ordinary sense, for here the patient is dying, and the only issue is the style of dying. *The Milk Train*, which Williams acknowledges "[has] been rightly described as an allegory and as a 'sophisticated fairy-tale.' " belongs roughly to the class of *Camino Real* of ten years earlier, though the roving panoramic style of *Camino Real* is replaced by a central focus on one character. She is a crass, wealthy old woman, a Mrs. Goforth ("it's my turn now to go forth," Williams makes her pun heavily in scene 6).

Here again Williams is on the *sic transit* theme that repeatedly attracts him, this time portraying a furiously fighting doomed person, like Big Daddy in *Cat on a Hot Tin Roof*, rather than the person who wilts away or seeks death. The treatment of a person dying amid opulence, protected by a gunman and savage dogs on a presumably impregnable height overlooking the Mediterranean, might remind different readers of Ivan Bunin's "The Gentleman from San Francisco" or Hugo von Hofmannsthal's *Everyman* or George Kaufman and Moss Hart's *You Can't Take It With You* or Aldous Huxley's *After Many a Summer*. Sissy Goforth, after a highly profitable career starting in a Georgia swamp and moving through the musical comedy stage to six husbands (a "Little Me" who has developed into a Claire Zachanassian of Duerrenmatt's *The Visit*), seems to think that you can take it with you; her heraldic device is the griffin, presumably an allusion to the mythic function of guarding gold in Scythia. There is a good deal of satire of that excessive love of property which reduces all other love to multiple sexual episodes; even on her deathbed Sissy, naked, summons a young man into her bedroom, with an ironic intimation of at least optical carnality. But though Sissy is a "dying monster," as her secretary Blackie calls her (an echo of *Sweet Bird of Youth*), she is more than an object of satire, for Williams also endows her with a brute sense of fact (within limits), an overwhelming candor (outside of specific areas of self-deceit), a blunt vulgarity not without its charm, and a passion for not being taken in.

The person who she thinks is intent on taking her in is a man in his thirties, Christopher Flanders, who has a number of times become a steady guest of well-to-do old ladies about to die and hence has become known as the "Angel of Death." This is Williams's latest, and most complex, version of the nurse or savior. Sissy sees in him only a hippie, a professional sponger, a pretended artist using "moral blackmail" on people who lack the "robust conscience" to throw him out as he deserves. The known facts about this partly mysterious figure make her estimate of him understandable, and he offers her assistance with a death-bedside manner that helps justify her doubts and scorn. Yet she does not want to lose him to a more vigorous old moneybags, the "Witch of Capri." Her doubleness of view either reflects or helps establish doubleness in him. In one stage direction, Williams refers to "the ambiguity of his character," and it appears that he could be an old ladies' con man ("you're suffering more than you need to," he tells Sissy, and he offers "agreeable companionship"), or "a saint of some kind" as Sissy jeeringly puts it, or a spiritual picaro, or something of all of these. Sissy sneers at his "list of suckers," and in a final burst of self-assertion she rejects him with "This milk train doesn't stop here any more"; this, along with her "I want to go forth alone," is quite convincing. On the other hand, she holds on to his hand as she dies. In using the term "Angel of Death" Williams may have in mind Azrael, which means "God has helped," for Chris says of his initial experience of this kind, "I had helped a dying old man to get through it," and his "Hindu teacher" replies "You've found your vocation." Chris tells Sissy, "you need somebody or something to mean God to you." It is possible that Chris is the bringer of "The Hidden God," to borrow Cleanth Brooks's title. When all the action takes place in a little world where, as Blackie says, "Everything signifies something," one notes Chris's name, the "Christ-bearer," and remembers that he arrives at Sissy's on foot, carrying an impressively heavy sack (it contains metalworking tools for making mobiles). He has some of the markings of Julian in Albee's *Tiny Alice*.

We have, then, ambiguity on both sides. Sissy is a heartless old miser, ruthless and paranoid; but her "fierce life" when dying and her tough grasp, if not of the whole human heart at least of the ways of the world, are not contemptible. She cannot let Chris go, but so suspects him that she half starves him while trying to use him. She may be a true stoic, a solitary endurer in a final scorning of illusions; or she may be a cheapskate trying to get needed help for nothing; or in her sardonic skepticism she may be utterly confused both about herself and him. Chris's epigram may have authority—"you're nobody's fool, but you're a fool"—or he may be skillful in working on her. Seen in the light of Sissy's combined attraction and repulsion, her need of help and her fear of quackery, Chris remains an ambiguous being who may be a professional "free loader" or a groundless consolation or a necessity or a blessing or the bearer of a "sense of reality" that is "disturbingly different" and hence has undeservedly made him, as he puts it, "a leper." The opulent world formally rejects him, crying fraud, but still clings to him, as if he were a man of indispensable vision—poet, artist, or prophet, false or true.

As a drama about the ways of dying, *Milk Train* belongs to the morality plays that are remarkably frequent in the modern theater, and as such it is peripherally related to tragedy. On the face of it, Sissy Goforth's struggle against death is rather like a melodramatic struggle against an omnipotent adversary raised to a level of significance and dignity; there is none of the pathos that such an action is likely to evoke. One of the bars against pathos is the uncertainty within Sissy herself; hence we may say that she has something of the tragic dividedness, even though it is present only because of the last-minute intrusion of motives that she hardly identifies or under-stands. There is not the primary split that is at the center of *Everyman*, the archetypal play about dying. But Williams is writing for a different world, and in *Milk Train* he avoids the errors of *Sweet Bird of Youth*—the sentimen-tality and the histrionics that the subject of death easily drives us into.

In general, we might reasonably think of Williams as experiencing a tension between fantasies of catastrophe and fantasies of salvation. Fantasies of catastrophe produce dramas of disaster; those of salvation may lead him to another basic structure of melodrama—twice, we note, with a *dea ex machina*. In *Milk Train* Williams works in another manner, that of allegory; here his interest is neither in catastrophe nor in the success or failure of the savior type, but in the complex attitudes of the affluent society toward the equivocal figure, artist or religious guide, who is both pensioner and alle-viator. If the dramatic focus is on the sick or disintegrating character who simply follows his sad downward course, or whose strongest act is to be the beneficiary of someone else's supporting clasp or cool hand on fevered brow, then the direction is not a tragic one. Nevertheless Williams shows himself also able to imagine the relatively well or strong person or that in-between figure who has had to struggle for wellness or strength. The last of these, Hannah Jelkes in *The Night of the Iguana*, is moving toward dramatic centrality. If such a character were to gain the center of the stage, it would be a move away from dramas of disaster.

THOMAS L. KING

Irony and Distance in The Glass Menagerie

Tennessee Williams's *The Glass Menagerie,* though it has achieved a firmly
established position in the canon of American plays, is often distorted, if
not misunderstood, by readers, directors, and audiences. The distortion
results from an overemphasis on the scenes involving Laura and Amanda
and their plight, so that the play becomes a sentimental tract on the trapped
misery of two women in St. Louis. This leads to the neglect of Tom's
soliloquies—speeches that can be ignored or discounted only at great peril,
since they occupy such a prominent position in the play. When not largely
ignored, they are in danger of being treated as nostalgic yearnings for a
former time. But they are not sentimental excursions into the past, paralleling
Amanda's, for while they contain sentiment and nostalgia, they also evince
a pervasive humor and irony and, indeed, form and contain the entire play.

Judging from the reviews, the distortion of the play began with the
original production. The reviews deal almost wholly with Laurette Taylor's
performance, making Amanda seem to be the principal character, and nearly
ignore the soliloquies. Even the passage of time has failed to correct this
tendency, for many later writers also force the play out of focus by pushing
Amanda forward. Among the original reviewers, Stark Young was one of
the few who recognized that the play is Tom's when he said: "The story
. . . all happens in the son's mind long afterward." He also recognized that
the production and Laurette Taylor tended to obscure the script, for, after
a lengthy discussion of Miss Taylor, he said, "But true as all this may be

From *Educational Theatre Journal* 25, no. 2 (May 1973). © 1973 by the American
Theatre Association, Inc.

of Miss Taylor, we must not let that blind us to the case of the play itself
and of the whole occasion." Young blamed on Eddie Dowling the failure of
the narration noted by others: "He speaks his Narrator scenes plainly and
serviceably by which, I think, they are made to seem to be a mistake on the
playwright's part, a mistake to include them at all; for they seem extraneous
and tiresome in the midst of the play's emotional current. If these speeches
were spoken with variety, impulse and intensity . . . the whole thing would
be another matter, truly a part of the story." Young indicates that while the
reviewers tended to neglect Tom and the soliloquies to concentrate on Laurette Taylor, they were encouraged to do so by a production which made the
play Amanda's.

The play, however, is not Amanda's. Amanda is a striking and a powerful character, but the play is Tom's. Tom opens the play and he closes it;
he also opens the second act and two further scenes in the first act—his is
the first word and the last. Indeed, Amanda, Laura, and the Gentleman
Caller do not appear in the play at all as separate characters. In a sense, as
Stark Young noted, Tom is the only character in the play, for we see not
the characters but Tom's memory of them—Amanda and the rest are merely
aspects of Tom's consciousness. Tom's St. Louis is not an objective one,
but a solipsist's created by Tom, the artist-magician, and containing Amanda,
Laura, and the Gentleman Caller. Tom is the Prospero of *The Glass Menagerie*,
and its world is the world of Tom's mind even more than *Death of a Salesman*'s
is the world of Willy Loman's mind. The play is warped and distorted when
any influence gives Amanda, Laura, or the glass menagerie any undue prominence. If Amanda looms large, she looms large in Tom's mind, not in her
own right: though of course the image that finally dominates Tom's mind
is that of Laura and the glass menagerie.

The full meaning of the scenes between the soliloquies lies not in themselves alone but also in the commentary provided by Tom standing outside
the scenes and speaking with reasonable candor to the audience and reader.
Moreover, the comment that the soliloquies makes is not a sentimental one;
that is, they are not only expressions of a wistful nostalgia for the lost,
doomed world of Amanda, Laura, and the glass menagerie but also contain
a good deal of irony and humor which work in the opposite direction. They
reveal Tom as an artist figure whose utterances show how the artist creates,
using the raw material of his own life.

The nature of the narrator's role as artist figure is indicated by Tom's
behavior in the scenes. He protects himself from the savage in-fighting in
the apartment by maintaining distance between himself and the pain of the
situation through irony. For example, when he gets into a fight with Amanda

in the third scene and launches into a long, ironic, and even humorous tirade—about how he "runs a string of cat-houses in the valley," how they call him "Killer, Killer Wingfield," how, on some occasions, he wears green whiskers—the irony is heavy and propels him out of the painful situation, out of the argument, and ultimately to the movies. Significantly, this scene begins with Tom writing, Tom the artist, and in it we see how the artistic sensibility turns a painful situation into "art" by using distance. In his verbal assault on his mother, Tom "creates" Killer Wingfield. Tom's ability to distance his experience, to protect himself from the debilitating atmosphere of the apartment makes him different from Laura. Laura does not have this refuge; she is unable to detach herself completely from the situation and she is destroyed by it. She does, of course, retreat to the glass menagerie and the Victrola, but this is the behavior of a severely disturbed woman. Her method of dealing with the situation, retreating into a "world of her own," does indeed, as Tom says, make her seem "just a little bit peculiar." Tom's method is more acceptable; he makes art.

The kind of contrast that exists between Laura and Tom is illustrated by a comment Jung made about James Joyce and his daughter, Lucia. Lucia had had a history of severe mental problems and, in 1934, she was put under the care of Jung. Discussing his patient and her famous father in a letter, Jung wrote: "His [Joyce's] 'psychological' style is definitely schizophrenic, with the difference, however, that the ordinary patient cannot help himself talking and thinking in such a way, while Joyce willed it and moreover developed it with all his creative forces, which incidentally explains why he himself did not go over the border. But his daughter did, because she was not a genius like her father, but merely a victim of her disease." On another occasion Jung said that the father and daughter "were like two people going to the bottom of a river, one falling and the other diving." We see here a psychoanalyst's perception of the problem of artist and non-artist which is much the same as the problem of Tom and Laura. Tennessee Williams's real-life sister, Rose, has also suffered from mental disturbances.

That an author's early play should contain a highly autobiographical character who shows the mechanism by which art is made out of the material of one's life is not particularly surprising, but it is a generally unnoted feature of *The Glass Menagerie* which is inextricably linked to the irony of the soliloquies. For the artist, irony is a device that protects him from the pain of his experience so that he may use it objectively in his art. We may suppose that Swift's irony shielded him from the dark view that he had of the world and that the failure of that irony brought on the madness that affected him at the end of his life. The artist needs his distance from the material of his art so that he may handle it objectively, and the soliloquies of *The Glass Menagerie*, in part, reveal the nature of that distance and how it is maintained.

Generally, each soliloquy oscillates between a sentimental memory of the past, which draws the narrator into it, and a wry irony which keeps him from being fully engulfed and controlled by it. This tension is found in all the soliloquies, though it is not always handled in the same way: sometimes the fond memory is predominant and sometimes the irony, but both are always present. At times, Tom seems almost deliberately to court disaster by creating for himself and the audience a memory so lovely and poignant that the pain of giving it up to return to reality is too much to bear, but return he does with mockery and a kind of wit that interrupts the witchery of memory just short of a withdrawn madness surrounded by soft music and a mind filled with "delicate rainbow colors." In short, Tom toys with the same madness in which his sister Laura is trapped but saves himself with irony.

The opening soliloquy begins on an ironic note. Tom says:

> Yes, I have tricks in my pocket, I have things up my sleeve. But I am the opposite of a stage magician. He gives you illusion that has the appearance of truth. I give you truth in the pleasant disguise of illusion.

These opening lines have a cocky tone—"I will trick you," Tom says, "I'll tell you that I'm going to trick you and I'll still do it even after you've been warned. Besides," he says with perhaps just a touch of derision, "you prefer trickery to the naked truth." Tom begins in the attitude of Whitman on the facing page of the first edition of *Leaves of Grass*—head thrown back, mocking, insolent, but not cruel.

Tom continues in the same mode by saying:

> To begin with, I turn back time. I reverse it to that quaint period, the thirties, when the huge middle class of America was matriculating in a school for the blind. Their eyes had failed them, or they had failed their eyes, and so they were having their fingers pressed forcibly down on the fiery Braille alphabet of a dissolving economy.
>
> In Spain there was revolution. Here there was only shouting and confusion. In Spain there was Guernica. Here there were disturbances of labor, sometimes pretty violent, in otherwise peaceful cities such as Chicago, Cleveland, Saint Louis . . .

To this point in the speech, Tom's principal mode is ironic, but as he moves on, though the irony remains, a stronger element of sentiment, of poignant memory creeps in. He begins to speak of memory and to enumerate the characters in the play:

> The play is memory. Being a memory play, it is dimly lighted,
> it is sentimental, it is not realistic. In memory everything seems
> to happen to music. That explains the fiddle in the wings.
>   I am the narrator of the play, and also a character in it. The
> other characters are my mother, Amanda, my sister, Laura, and
> a gentleman caller who appears in the final scenes.

The only break in this poignant mood is the phrase "that explains the fiddle in the wings"—an unfortunate phrase, but demonstrative of the tension, of the rhythmic swing back and forth between sweet nostalgia and bitter irony. The play may be sentimental rather than realistic, but "that explains the fiddle in the wings" breaks the sentiment.

Tom continues by saying:

> He [the gentleman caller] is the most realistic character in the
> play, being an emissary from a world of reality that we were
> somehow set apart from. But since I have a poet's weakness for
> symbols, I am using this character also as a symbol; he is the
> long delayed but always expected something that we live for.

With these words, the narrator drops his ironic detachment and enters into the mood of memory. The words can hardly be delivered but as in a reverie, in a deep reflection, the voice coming out of a man who, after frankly acknowledging the audience at the beginning of the speech, has now sunk far into himself so that the audience seems to overhear his thoughts. He then shakes off the mood with a return to irony and makes a kind of joke:

> There is a fifth character in the play who doesn't appear except
> in this larger-than-life-size photograph over the mantel. This is
> our father who left us a long time ago. He was a telephone man
> who fell in love with long distances; he gave up his job with the tele-
> phone company and skipped the light fantastic out of town . . .
>   The last we heard of him was a picture post-card from
> Mazatlan, on the Pacific coast of Mexico, containing a message
> of two words—"Hello—Good-bye!" and no address.

There is humor here—not sentiment and not sentimental humor. Tom speaks fondly of his mother and sister and remembers their lost lives and the gentleman caller who symbolizes the loss and the failure, and we can imagine that his gaze becomes distant and withdrawn as he allows himself to be carried away into the memory, but then he remembers another member of the family, the father, and that hurts too much to give in to so he shakes off the reverie and returns once more to irony. The irony is no longer the playful irony of the interlocutor before the audience, but an irony which protects him from the painful memories of the past, that allows him to rise superior to the "father who left us" and to get a laugh from the audience, for the audience should and will chuckle at the end of the opening soliloquy as the light fades on Tom and he leaves his seaman's post. The chuckle may be good-natured, but the humor is not; it is gallows humor in which the condemned man asserts himself before a crowd in relation to which he is horribly disadvantaged by making it laugh. Tom is in control of his memory and already he is beginning to endeavor to work his trick by manipulating the audience's mood.

The opening soliloquy, then, reveals a number of elements that are to be important in the play: it establishes a tension between sentimental nostalgia and detached irony as well as a narrator who is to function as stage magician. The narrator disavows this, but we cannot take him at his word. He says that he is the opposite of a stage magician, but only because his truth looks like illusion rather than the other way round; he is still the magician who creates the play. He says that the play is sentimental rather than realistic, but that is a half truth, for while it contains large doses of sentiment, for the narrator at least, irony sometimes quenches the sentiment. Indeed, Irving Babbit's phrase describing romantic irony is appropriate here: "Hot baths of sentiment . . . followed by cold douches of irony."

The dominant note of the second soliloquy, at the beginning of the third scene, is irony. In the first soliloquy, Tom has provided the audience with a poignant picture of Laura and Amanda cut off from the world "that we were somehow set apart from." In the second soliloquy, irony almost completely obliterates the poignance as we see Amanda at work trying to find a gentleman caller for Laura, a gentleman caller who is "like some archetype of the universal unconscious." Tom continues the irony as he says:

> She began to take logical steps in the planned direction.
> Late that winter and in the early spring—realizing that extra money would be needed to properly feather the nest and plume the bird—she conducted a vigorous campaign on the telephone, roping in subscribers to one of those magazines for matrons called *The Home-maker's Companion*, the type of journal that features the

serialized sublimations of ladies of letters who think in terms of delicate cup-like breasts, slim, tapering waists, rich, creamy thighs, eyes like wood-smoke in autumn, fingers that soothe and caress like strains of music, bodies as powerful as Etruscan sculpture.

The mocking humor in this is revealed by the derisive alliteration, the hyperbolic language, and in the humorous, parodying evocation of all the clichés of these stories. The speech makes fun of the literary equivalents of Amanda's memories of gentleman callers in the mythical South. This is not to say that Amanda is savagely attacked with a kind of Swiftian irony; nevertheless, the attack is there, though the irony is balanced somewhat by one irruption of the nostalgic, pitying mode of discourse when Tom says that even when the gentleman caller was not mentioned "his presence hung in mother's preoccupied look and in my sister's frightened, apologetic manner." The irony is also humorous and gets a laugh from audiences if it is performed as irony— especially at the end of the speech where, just as the first soliloquy breaks into a mild humor at the end, Tom humorously parodies the magazine stories.

The first soliloquy strikes a balance between irony and nostalgia, the second is primarily ironic, and the third is primarily nostalgic. The third soliloquy begins with the Paradise Dance Hall:

Across the alley from us was the Paradise Dance Hall. On evenings in spring the windows and doors were open and the music came outdoors. Sometimes the lights were turned out except for a large glass sphere that hung from the ceiling. It would turn slowly about and filter the dusk with delicate rainbow colors.

Rainbow colors, in fact, fill much of the play: in the scene with Laura, late at night, after Tom has returned from the movies, the magic scarf he produces is rainbow-colored—this is one of the few scenes in which Tom and Laura relate tenderly to one another; the Paradise Dance Hall filters the dusk with "delicate rainbow colors"; sex hangs "in the gloom like a chandelier" and floods the world with "brief, deceptive rainbows"; and, in the last soliloquy, Tom says that he sometimes passes the window of a shop where perfume is sold—"The window is filled with pieces of colored glass, tiny transparent bottles in delicate colors like bits of a shattered rainbow." In the third soliloquy, the Paradise Dance Hall provides the rainbow colors that fill and transform the alley. The irony breaks through in only a few places: when Tom disrupts the mood of magic by pointing out that you could see the young couples "kissing behind ash-pits and telephone poles," and, as usual, at the end when he says, "All the world was waiting for bombardments."

All three soliloquies in the first act work together to help define its movement. The first soliloquy is fairly well balanced between nostalgia and irony. The detached irony of the second soliloquy foreshadows Tom's struggle to detach himself from his situation; after it Tom fights with his mother and leaves to go to the movies. The third soliloquy asserts the nostalgic mode, and the scene following this, in which Tom and Amanda talk of the gentleman caller, is a tender, loving one. We see a playful, warm scene between Tom and his mother out on the fire escape which shows how, in spite of their quarrels, Tom and Amanda could also have their warm, understanding moments. By the end of the first act, the audience should be taken in by Tom's trick, drawn into the rainbow-colored world and the pleasant memory of past times. The pain of Tom's memory has been repudiated in the second soliloquy with irony, and, after the fight, when Tom runs off to the movies, with the delicate nostalgia of the third soliloquy, flooding the stage with rainbow light. The trick is working—we begin to think that Tom and his mother will get along after all, that a gentleman caller will come to rescue them, but it remains a trick wrought by the magic of the rainbow which is broken, whose colors are "deceptive."

The second act begins with a soliloquy which, like the first, strikes something of a balance between irony and nostalgia. Tom begins with a description of Jim in language that indicates that he has a genuine kind of amazed liking for this Irish boy. Only gentle irony is present in the following words:

> In high school, Jim was a hero. He had tremendous Irish good
> nature and vitality with the scrubbed and polished look of white
> chinaware. He seemed to move in a continual spotlight. He was
> a star in basketball, captain of the debating club, president of the
> senior class and the glee club, and he sang the male lead in the
> annual light operas. He was always running or bounding, never
> just walking. He seemed always at the point of defeating the law
> of gravity.

Jim is made light of by the phrases "white chinaware" and "defeating the law of gravity," but the mockery is mild, though it becomes stronger as the speech continues:

> He was shooting with such velocity through his adolescence that
> you would logically expect him to arrive at nothing short of the
> White House by the time he was thirty. But Jim apparently ran
> into more interference after his graduation from Soldan. His

speed had definitely slowed. Six years after he left high school he was holding a job that wasn't much better than mine.

The irony begins to break through even more strongly after these words, for Tom was "valuable to him as someone who could remember his former glory, who had seen him win basketball games and the silver cup in debating." And the irony even cuts against Tom: "He knew of my secret practice of retiring to a cabinet of the wash-room to work on poems whenever business was slack in the warehouse." A degree of bitterness begins to emerge when Tom says that, with the example of Jim, the other boys began to smile at him too, "as people smile at some oddly fashioned dog that trots across their path at some distance." The bitterness is quickly moderated, however, when Tom sympathetically remembers his sister in high school: "In high school Laura was as unobtrusive as Jim was astonishing." Finally, as always in these soliloquies, the speech ends with an ironic barb that can often draw a laugh from the audience. Tom says that when he asked Jim home to dinner "he grinned and said, 'You know, Shakespeare, I never thought of you as having folks!' He was about to discover that I did. . . ."

The culmination of all the soliloquies and of the tension between irony and nostalgia that is carefully developed in them, is in the final one. Tom's last speech contains just two touches of ironic detachment, but these are critical and are the foci on which this speech and, indeed, for Tom, the whole play turns. The speech begins with a touch of ironic humor. In the preceding scene, Amanda has told Tom to go to the moon. He begins his final speech with "I didn't go to the moon." This is a decidedly humorous line, indicating that Tom still has access to his detachment, but the audience is not laughing anymore, its detachment has been broken down. The speech then quickly moves into a tone of lyric regret:

> I didn't go to the moon, I went much further—for time is the longest distance between two places. Not long after that I was fired for writing a poem on the lid of a shoe-box. I left Saint Louis. I descended the steps of this fire-escape for a last time and followed, from then on, in my father's footsteps, attempting to find in motion what was lost in space. I traveled around a great deal. The cities swept about me like dead leaves, leaves that were brightly colored but torn away from the branches. I would have stopped, but I was pursued by something. It always came upon me unawares, taking me altogether by surprise. Perhaps it was a familiar bit of music. Perhaps it was only a piece of transparent glass. Perhaps I am walking along a street at night, in some strange

94   THOMAS L. KING

city, before I have found companions. I pass the lighted window
of a shop where perfume is sold. The window is filled with pieces
of colored glass, tiny transparent bottles in delicate colors, like
bits of a shattered rainbow. Then all at once my sister touches
my shoulder. I turn around and look into her eyes. Oh, Laura,
Laura, I tried to leave you behind me, but I am more faithful
than I intended to be! I reach for a cigarette, I cross the street,
I run into the movies or a bar, I buy a drink, I speak to the
nearest stranger—anything that can blow your candles out!

For nowadays the world is lit by lightning! Blow out your
candles, Laura—and so good-bye.

The irony in this passage is no longer humorous. When Tom says "I didn't
go to the moon," no one is laughing, and the final, ironic "and so good-bye"
is not even potentially humorous. Tom seems to have been captured by the
memory and the audience has almost certainly been captured, but Tom, in
the end, still has his detachment. Laura's candles go out and Tom is relieved
of his burden, uttering a final, flip farewell, but the audience has been more
faithful than it intended to be; they are left behind, tricked by Tom who is
free for the moment while they must face their grief, their cruelty, for they
are the world that the Wingfields were somehow set apart from, they are
the ones who shattered the rainbow.

The soliloquies, then, are of a piece: they all alternate between sentiment
and irony, between mockery and nostalgic regret, and they all end with an
ironic tag, which, in most cases, is potentially humorous. They show us the
artist manipulating his audience, seeming to be manipulated himself to draw
them in, but in the end resuming once more his detached stance. When Tom
departs, the audience is left with Laura and Amanda alone before the dead,
smoking candles, and Tom escapes into his artist's detachment having ex-
orcized the pain with the creation of the play. This is the trick that Tom
has in his pocket.

JAMES COAKLEY

Time and Tide on the Camino Real

Among the plays of Tennessee Williams *Camino Real* remains an enigma. A failure on Broadway, subjected to drastic revision as if its author refused to let it ever congeal into some finished form, and regarded by its critics as no more than the reworking of a *jeu d'esprit*, it received, Williams tells us, "more conscious attention to form and construction than . . . any work before." Well and good, we might say, but after decades of exposure to European experimentalists, audiences are still baffled by, indeed scornful of, this fascinating and demanding play.

One need not invoke esthetics, literary theory, or that tiresomely incantatory phrase "avant-garde" to see that *Camino Real* is a different kind of play. Its persistent dramatic method is via the sharpest possible contrast and juxtaposition of style. Indeed, stylistic disparity promotes the play's bold efforts to break loose from the stage and spill into the house, enhancing the dramatic action's reliance upon theatricalist conventions (mime, dance, and lavish technical effects) as the source of the drama's attempts to plunge the audience directly into its reality. Yet, this eclecticism of method does not mean that the piece's structure is loose, flimsy, or haphazard. On the contrary, in no play of Williams before or since does his sense of form, or where he is going and how he is going there, serve him more faithfully.

Camino Real is nonlinear in structure, and the use of such a pattern immediately prescribes hard and fast rules: (1) to relinquish forward movement of narrative and action is to lose the easy tension in the rigidly selective

From *Tennessee Williams: A Tribute*, edited by Jac Tharpe. © 1977 by the University Press of Mississippi.

organization common to linear drama where one event plunges irreversibly
onto the next; (2) to deny the melodramatic core of such an action is to reject
what Ionesco (see *Victims of Duty*) calls, for example, the "detective story"
nature of drama; (3) and, finally, to deal in episodic units (Williams calls
them "blocks," or, more familiarly, French scenes) is to present experience
as fragmented, often seemingly aimless or ambiguous. This fragmentation
of experience (common to films, but risky business in the theater) suggests
the momentary focus on the instant, the episode caught in time and frozen
in space, in which we are permitted to discover in vertical movement layers
of personality often impossible to consider in the linear form's horizontal
progression. In theory, at least, the nonlinear mode chooses to linger in the
hidden corners of human motivation, where behavior has the clarity of true
complexity. Finally, the most serious challenge of this play is its refusal to
accept time either as sequential or as the fundamental common denominator
of human affairs. To achieve this immediacy it presents time as discursive,
arbitrary, and above all subjective. This particularly modern notion of time
is the organizing principle of *Camino Real*, a method perfectly suited to the
presentational production style which should, as Williams insists, aim for
the freedom of improvisation in performance. It should give that sense of
the "perpetual present" where the play is poised, in the words of Thornton
Wilder, on a "razor-edge, between past and future, which is the essential
character of the conscious being."

So restless a method as fluidity, however, requires control over the
diffuse vignettes sprawling across the stage. To absorb an audience in a free
association of disconnected images invites chaos or, worse, the private vision
of a dilettante. Williams is too shrewdly in control of his materials, however,
too aware of the dangers of excessive fragmentation, to allow his play to
wander off in meaningless montages. To be sure, time interiorized and
discontinuous provides unity, but *Camino* resides paradoxically in the best
of two possible worlds: bracketed by Don Quixote's dream, its interior
plunges ceaselessly across the country of the mind revealing a completely
subjective spectrum of colors, shapes, and images, while retaining a semblance of direction in the adventures of its three quasiheroes, the Don, Kilroy,
and Lord Byron. Melodramatic considerations suggesting progressions and
resolutions bristle within the play's busy frame, but the truth is that while,
much in the fashion of Chekhov, the arrivals and departures of characters
imply movement to a destination, they really lead to perpetual wandering
(the Don and Kilroy), or to death (Lord Byron). This trio is as rootless and
spiritually displaced as any who are trapped forever on the Camino.

The effect of this calculated disorder upon characterization, however, allows for the play's most remarkable achievement. Normally, theatricalism robs character of dimension and consistency; tends, in fact, to dehumanize. In *Camino*, it seems to me, Williams withstands any impulses to present his people as mere style with no matter. Avoiding traditional treatment of his gallery of familiar literary types, he does rely on overtones, the suggestions of myth surrounding them, but in no way are they simply dusted off, refurbished, and reused. They are deployed and developed solely in terms of their perception of time. The persistent contrast is what they once were with what they are now: Quixote is an old desert rat, Casanova an impoverished, seedy roué, and Marguerite Gautier a frightened and lonely woman, addicted to drugs. Here, indeed, is the nub of the drama: the stasis of the present vs. the motion promised by the future, both of which are frustrated by the past's refusal to disappear. For time halted does not erase memory; it encourages the reflection proper to dimensioned characterization. The characters can be understood only by what we might call reflexive reference, their passions and problems darting back and forth; and, like the heroes of Pirandello, condemned to the limbo of the present, they are able to summon nonsequential, past experiences on the instant.

Three groups inhabit the Camino: the outcasts—the bums and drunks of a flophouse; the decadents—Marguerite Gautier, Jacques Casanova, and the Baron de Charlus; and the idealists—Don Quixote, Kilroy, and Lord Byron. Each is tainted (humanized) by the problem of time's meaning; each is dramatized (rather than merely represented) downward to the essence of human existence, forced to examine his problems in the arrested depths of the moment. External reality, the movement of life from point to point, is rejected, for the truth is to be discovered only in context, only in the fusion of past, present, and future: and amalgam of hurts, questions, and no answers. The outcasts (technically they also provide background) elect to ignore time, escaping into drugs and alcohol; for them life is a scavenger hunt "in a bazaar where the human heart is part of the bargain." There is no struggle—nothing in fact, but the cynical acceptance of things as they are. The sentimental comfort of memories is useless; the satisfaction of appetites is all that remains; and the moral principle is all too clear; indifference to time, to the world, in effect, breeds disaster, self-destruction. To shirk the issue is to end up, as Casanova does, on Skid Row, life hastily collected in a battered portmanteau.

But the decadents, the transients of an expensive tourist hotel, are, like all practicing romantics, terrified of time. Anguished over past glories and present stalemate, their attainment of spiritual freedom (the original reason for their rebellion against the world's order) is movement, flight, escape from the immobility of the Camino. They are morally, however, no better than their counterparts across the plaza. Practicing the same vices, they have more money, but the same fears. And for them to contemplate temporality in human affairs is only to see existence as no more than a series of waystations towards death. With these characters, as we might expect, are posed the play's most serious questions in set speeches of important thematic weight; the chance, as Williams sees it, to play upon his central perception: life is no more than "dim, communal comfort" eroded by change; values are illusory, perpetually in transit. How, in short, is one to live? It is a despair worthy of Beckett, priding itself upon no more than the black honesty of its vision. Neither psychological in origin (as in *Streetcar*) nor diluted with the panacea of the social worker preaching adjustment to the human condition, this despair is metaphysical and profoundly moral. Suspended and viewed in the pity and terror common to all, it is not sentimental; it is artistic, it seems to me, its logic and worth predicated upon the givens of the structure in which it operates. Indeed, in block ten, a brief scene between Marguerite and Jacques, Williams drops the theatricalist mask and allows his heroine to proclaim the dilemma correctly:

> What are we sure of ? Not even of our existence, dear comforting friend! And whom can we ask the questions that torment us? "What is this place?" "Where are we?"

In the microcosm of the moment all is visible; character, in effect, becomes symbol, the inner life of these people bursts forth, projecting the scope of the play outward to an indictment not only of the world of the play but of a universe equally perverse and corrupt.

The idealists do retain symbols of past achievements (Byron's pen, Kilroy's Golden Gloves, Quixote's blue ribbon), but each chooses, despite the consequences, merely to depart into life against time's ravages. Each makes that deliberate and existential choice by which the self is defined in this world. Yet the promise of self-fulfillment is slight. The Don does forbid Kilroy the pleasures of self-pity, and his only answer to the dilemma is that we must smile, making the best of what we have. To do less is immoral.

Thematically and structurally, then, *Camino* is a most ambitious play; or rather, a scenario, as Williams says, fit only for the "vulgarity of performance." One need not become its apologist to see that its intention and execution are evenly matched. To deprecate it as the triumph of the theatrical over the literary imagination is to miss the most important of matters: its form is its meaning, its central perceptions are stated directly, sincerely, and insistently: a dark message in the garish colors of a circus sideshow.

ARTHUR GANZ

A Desperate Morality

The true setting for the plays of Wilde and Synge is the world of art, a refuge from the forces most gravely threatening to them: Victorian philistinism in one case, ultimate mortality in the other. But a different response is devised for troubling demands by Tennessee Williams and Arthur Miller, even though their affinities with these unlikely predecessors are significant. Usually thought of together only because they are contemporaries who dominated the American theater in the years following World War II, Williams and Miller, despite notable differences in style and substance, were finally making the same attempt: to create in their works a metaphorical "world" that would be shelter for the self against the assaults of a hostile reality. But for Williams and Miller this sanctuary is not a world of art but a world of innocence. Like the other visionary worlds we have been considering, this one, too, is occasionally seen as a literal place, but it is always and essentially a psychic condition, in this case freedom from an encroaching sense of guilt. That questions of innocence and guilt are central to the work of Arthur Miller, whose plays are filled with ethical crises, has been evident from the first; it is, however, a good deal less obvious in the case of Tennessee Williams.

To call him a moralist might seem to bestow a strange appellation on a playwright whose works deal so sensationally with rape, castration, cannibalism, and other bizarre activities. But in examining the plays of Tennessee Williams it is exactly this point—that he wishes to judge the self, not

From *Realms of the Self: Variations on a Theme in Modern Drama.* © 1980 by New York University. New York University Press, 1980.

analyze it—that must be borne in mind. The world of Williams's plays, though it is founded on his observations of the American South, is essentially an inner world dominated by certain overpowering obsessions: fear, loneliness, death, sexuality, and above all innocence and guilt. In this special world the self struggles to affirm its innocence, but over and over again it is adjudged guilty.

Admittedly, Williams's morality is a curious one, but it is a consistent ethic, giving him a point of view from which he can make his judgments. Yet to say that Williams rewards those who, by his standards, are virtuous and punishes those who are wicked is to oversimplify, for in Williams's plays good often has an unexpected affinity with evil. Beneath the skin of the Christlike martyr destroyed by the cruel forces of death and sterility lies the disease, the transgression that had made the author destroy him, while the character most fiercely condemned may at the same time be the one for whom pardon is most passionately demanded. From the self-lacerating desire simultaneously to praise and to punish stems the violence that agitates so many of Williams's plays.

To understand this violence in Williams's work we must first look at his gentlest plays, those in which the virtuous self is rewarded, for here is most directly revealed the morality by which the guilty one is later so terribly condemned. Surprisingly, one of Williams's most significant plays is an indifferent and undramatic one-acter about the death of D. H. Lawrence, only slightly redeemed by the audacious title, *I Rise in Flame, Cried the Phoenix*. The play is so important because it gives us the central fact we must have to understand Williams's work, the nature of his literary parentage.

Whether or not Williams assesses Lawrence correctly is, for an understanding of Williams's own work, irrelevant. What does matter here is that at a very early point in his career (*I Rise in Flame* dates from 1941) Williams saw Lawrence as the great writer who "celebrates the body" and himself apparently as that writer's disciple. But a disciple is not invariably the best advocate of his master's doctrine; Williams began his career as a neo-Lawrentian writer by basing a very bad play on one of Lawrence's short stories. Called *You Touched Me* (also the title of Lawrence's story), this early work (copyrighted in 1942), of slight interest in itself, is revelatory in the distortions it introduces while transforming the original material and additionally important for establishing a structural pattern that Williams was later to use far more effectively.

Williams's play (written in collaboration with Donald Windham) becomes a stunning vulgarization of Lawrence's tale as the younger sister of the story, Emmie, is changed into a frigid maiden aunt representing "aggressive sterility," and the heroine, Matilda, a thin, large-nosed woman of thirty-two in Lawrence's version, is turned into a pale girl of twenty, the cliché of the frail, sheltered maiden. Hadrian, in the story a neat, scheming little soldier with a common-looking mustache, is transformed into "a clean-cut, muscular young man in the dress uniform of a lieutenant in the Royal Canadian Air Force," much given to speeches about faith, the glories of the future, and the conquering of new countries of the mind. And finally, the elderly pottery manufacturer is turned into a spry, if alcoholic old sea captain. Given this set of popular-magazine characters, the play has no trouble reaching its predictable conclusion as the captain helps the handsome airman defeat the aunt and win the shy Matilda.

What is significant is not that at this early stage in his career, Williams should write a poor play, but that, while retaining the essential Lawrentian theme, he should so alter Lawrence's material as to produce an unmistakable Tennessee Williams play. The light but subtle characterizations around which Lawrence built his story are in the play coarsened to the point where the characters are obviously marked out simply as good and bad. Williams here is very little of a psychologist; rather, he is a moralist, a special kind of sexual moralist, whose creations are judged virtuous only if they owe their allegiance to the sexual impulse. Although Williams distorted and sentimentalized Lawrence's story, its central action—the awakening to life, and particularly to sexual life, of one who had previously been dead to it—was one that Williams, with an unquestioning faith in romantic vitalism, saw as profoundly good. Developed roughly in *You Touched Me*, it was then placed at the center of two of his most pleasing works, *The Glass Menagerie* and *The Rose Tattoo*. In each of these plays a woman who has retired from life is confronted by a man, like Hadrian, the sexual force designed to release her from bondage. But whereas he succeeds in one case, in the other he fails. The reasons for this difference are worth noting.

The figure of Laura in *The Glass Menagerie* has clearly been developed from that of Matilda in *You Touched Me*, who is described by Williams as having "the delicate, almost transparent quality of glass." Both are shy, fragile creatures, remote from the life around them. But whereas Hadrian awakens Matilda to life, Laura's gentleman caller gives her only a momentary glimpse of normal existence before she drifts back into the fantasy world of glass animals. Although in Williams's moral system the rejection of life is a crime demanding punishment, Laura is adjudged innocent; she is not frigid and hostile; she does not reject but rather is rejected, not because of her limp, which does not exist in "Portrait of a Girl in Glass," Williams's own short story upon which he based his play, but because she is the sensitive, misunderstood exile, a recurrent character in Williams's work, one of the fugitive kind, who are too fragile to face a malignant reality and must have a special world in which they can take shelter. The vigorous Serafina Delle Rose of *The Rose Tattoo*, however, deliberately rejects life after the death of her husband, leading an existence as solitary and sterile as that of Laura among the glass animals. Fortunately, when the truck driver Alvaro Mangiacavallo, who has the face of a clown but the body of her husband, appears, she escapes guilt by disclaiming her rejection, returning to the world of life, and accepting sexuality again.

A later and less likable work, *Period of Adjustment* belongs with this group of gentle dramas, for at its conclusion the two couples are permitted to enter the haven of sexual harmony as the phallically named community of High Point sinks farther into the cavern beneath it. But before the playwright allows these consummations, each of the two men who are its central figures is humiliated and forced to admit his guilt. They have been great fighters and war heroes, but one has abased himself to marry for money, and the other has rejected his homosexual nature or at least pretended to a virility he does not possess. Ultimately the play collapses because the author, vaguely hostile to his masculine characters, cannot decide whether they are to be forgiven or punished.

Although Williams's impulse to forgive and grant entrance to the realm of innocence has produced attractive plays, his need to punish has led to his most powerful work. Invariably, the central crime in Williams's moral code has been that from which Matilda and Serafina were preserved, the rejection of life. The theme of punishment for an act of rejection is at the center of a group of plays very different from that already examined, but it is expressed most explicitly in a short story, "Desire and the Black Masseur," from the volume *One Arm and Other Stories*. In this story the central character, Walter Burns, who has yielded to the loveless life around him, is haunted by a nameless desire that is fulfilled only by the manipulations of a gigantic black masseur who first beats Burns and then, as the story veers toward fantasy, kills him and proceeds to eat his body in the atmosphere of a sacred ritual. Bizarre, perhaps a little ridiculous,the story nevertheless makes of its hero a broad symbol of human guilt and desire for atonement. Claiming that the sins of the world "are really only its partialities, its incompletions, and these are what sufferings must atone for," Williams attempts to suggest a wider vision comprehending the world and the place of suffering in it. "And meantime," he concludes, "slowly, with barely a thought of so doing, the earth's whole population twisted and writhed beneath the manipulation of night's black fingers, the white ones of day with skeletons splintered and flesh reduced to pulp, as out of this unlikely problem, the answer, perfection, was slowly evolved through torture."

We need not believe that anything like perfection could be evolved from the process described here (nor linger over the element of erotic gratification in these masochistic images) to see its significance in relation to Williams's major work. The story concerns an elaborate, ritual punishment of one who has rejected life and, more specifically, rejected sexuality. A whole group of plays including some of the most remarkable—*A Streetcar Named Desire*, *Summer and Smoke*, *Cat on a Hot Tin Roof*, and *Suddenly Last Summer*—centers not only on Williams's refusal to grant the world of refuge sought by so many of his characters but on his inflicting terrible punishments for sexual rejection, for him an act synonymous with the rejection of life itself.

The stage action of *A Streetcar Named Desire*, still Williams's best play, consists almost entirely of the punishment its heroine endures—even as she desperately seeks a place of safety—as atonement for her central act of rejection, her sin in terms of Williams's morality. Since Williams begins the action of his play at a late point in the story, the act itself is not played out on stage but only referred to. Unaware that she is describing the crime that condemns her, Blanche tells Mitch of her discovery that her adored young husband was a homosexual and of the consequences of her disgust and revulsion:

> BLANCHE: . . . He'd stuck the revolver into his mouth, and
> fired—so that the back of his head had been—blown
> away! (*She sways and covers her face.*) It was because—on
> the dance floor—unable to stop myself—I'd suddenly
> said—"I saw! I know! You disgust me . . . " And then the
> searchlight which had been turned on the world was
> turned off again and never for one moment since has there
> been any light that's stronger than this—kitchen—candle.

While Blanche delivers this speech and the ones surrounding it, the polka to which she and her husband had danced, the Varsouviana, sounds in the background. At the end of the play, when Blanche sees the Doctor who is to lead her off to the dubious refuge of the asylum, her punishment is complete and the Varsouviana sounds again, linking her crime to its retribution. As Blanche flees from the Doctor, "the Varsouviana is filtered into a weird distortion accompanied by the cries and noises of the jungle." These symbolize both Blanche's chaotic state and the instrument of her destruction, Stanley Kowalski, the complete sensual animal, the equivalent in function to the black masseur.

Although Kowalski's primary mission, to destroy Blanche, is clear, his role evokes certain ambiguities. By becoming Blanche's destroyer, he also becomes the avenger of her homosexual husband. Although he is Williams's exaggeration of the Lawrentian lover, it is appropriate from Williams's point of view that Kowalski should to some degree be identified with the lonely homosexual who had been driven to suicide, for Williams saw Lawrence not only as the propagandist of sexual vitality but as the symbol of the solitary, rejected exile. (In the poem called "Cried the Fox" from Williams's collection, *In the Winter of Cities*, Lawrence is seen as the fox pursued by the cruel hounds.) But however gratifying it may be to identify the embodiment of admired male sexuality with the exile artist and thus by implication with the exile homosexual, the identification, even for Williams, remains tenuous.

Though an avenger, Kowalski is as guilty of destroying Blanche as she is of destroying her husband. For Blanche, who has lost the plantation Belle Reve, the beautiful dream world of safety and gracious gentility, is an exile like the homosexual; her tormentor, the apelike Kowalski, from one point of view the representative of Lawrentian vitality, is from another the brutal, male torturer of a lonely spirit. But however much she wishes to find herself safe and see herself as innocent, Blanche remains, in Williams's moral vision, guilty, unworthy of rescue. She has in effect killed her husband by her cruelty, and her belated acknowledgment of sexuality, turning away from death to its opposite that she had so denied—"the opposite is desire," as Blanche herself says—leads only to her ultimate destruction.

Although a variant on the act of rejection is performed in *Summer and Smoke*, guilt is not absolute and punishment is mitigated. The heroine is similar to those already encountered: the frail, spinsterish southern girl with her sensuality repressed by a puritanical background. Like many of Williams's characters, the hero needs love as an escape from solitude: at one point, while giving Alma an ironic anatomy lecture, he shouts, "This part down here is the sex which is hungry for love because it is sometimes lonesome." At the crucial moment she refuses his advances and rushes off. Alma, having committed the sin of rejection, is condemned, as Blanche was before her, to be tormented by the very urges she had fled from and to turn to promiscuity. Yet because her sin has been somewhat diminished by her realization of it, there is a suggestion at the end of the play that the traveling salesman she has picked up may lead her to salvation rather than destruction.

Like *Summer and Smoke*, a later play, *The Night of the Iguana*, has affinities with both the severity of *Streetcar* and the gentleness of *The Glass Menagerie*. Its heroine, Hannah Jelkes, a New England spinster artist, is like Blanche confronted by an appeal for help from one with abnormal sexual inclinations (a homosexual in Williams's original story but converted for stage purposes to an unfrocked minister with a taste for pubescent girls). But instead of driving him to suicide, she offers him what limited help she can. Because like Laura and Alma she is too delicate and repressed to take on a full emotional relationship, Shannon's rescue is finally left to the sexually vital hotel proprietor, while Hannah must continue in loveless solitude. By her sympathy for Shannon and for the pathetic fetishist she had previously aided, she has earned, however, a fate far gentler than the breakdown meted out to Blanche and to her own predecessor in the source story.

In *Cat on a Hot Tin Roof*, however, Williams produces something much nearer the pattern of *Streetcar*. In fact, from one point of view *Cat* is simply a reworking of the materials of the earlier play, but with a crucial change that made it almost impossible for Williams to bring his new play to a reasonable conclusion. Again, the motivating figure, who does not appear on stage, is the rejected homosexual; the rejector, whose youth like Blanche's is fading, has also like Blanche turned to drink, attempting to find a sheltered world in a state of alcoholic dissociation. But because the one who has rejected, the sinner who must atone, is not a woman but a man, certain problems arise. The audience, although it sympathizes with Blanche, can accept her as guilty. She could not only have given her husband love instead of contempt but at least the possibility of a heterosexual life. But, confronted with Skipper's telephoned confession of a homosexual attachment, Brick has fewer possibilities before him. The audience is likely to feel that sympathetic understanding is the most that Brick can offer—short of admitting to a similar inclination. Yet Williams, although he is ambiguous about several points in this play, is not ambiguous about Brick's guilt. Big Daddy himself, who despises mendacity, condemns his son. "You! dug the grave of your friend," he cries, "and kicked him in it!—before you'd face the truth with him!" But it is beyond Big Daddy's power to tell Brick just what he was to do.

In a play designed for the commercial theater, Williams could not at that time openly punish Brick for failing to be an honest homosexual. When he showed *Cat* to the representative of that theater, Elia Kazan, and Kazan suggested certain changes, Williams accepted his advice. As a result, the comparatively optimistic third act performed on Broadway contains the shift in Brick's character that leads to the possibility that his sexual quiescence, a symbolic castration suggested by his broken ankle, will not be permanent. There is no reason to disbelieve Williams's claim that he had agreed to Kazan's suggestions to retain his interest, but it is worth noting that by mitigating Brick's suffering Williams was relieved of the necessity of asking his audience to agree that Brick deserved punishment for an act much of that audience would not have considered reprehensible.

Although the tentativeness of Williams's condemnation of Brick makes it difficult to know whether Brick was so condemned for rejecting his homosexual friend or for rejecting his own homosexual nature, in *Cat*, at least, homosexuality itself carries no stigma. Although Big Daddy is a man of almost ostentatious virility (the latent antifeminism in his sexual revulsion from Big Mama is not stressed) as well as the most powerful and sympathetic figure in the play, he had served and respected the two idyllically conceived homosexuals, Straw and Ochello, and received his land from them as a kind of benediction. Yet in *Suddenly Last Summer*, a later play of what may be called the "punishment" group, Williams has produced a work in which the homosexual—so often for him the symbol of the lonely, rejected exile—becomes the rejector, the sinner who must be punished.

But neither this shift in Williams's usual pattern nor the *bizarrerie* of the play's atmosphere should conceal the fact that *Suddenly Last Summer* follows closely the structure of the other plays in this group. Once more the pivotal figure, the exile homosexual, has met a violent death before the opening of the play. As the sterile Brick is contrasted with Big Daddy, the life-giving father of *Cat*, so the cruel Sebastian is played off against the loving and merciful Catharine who gives herself not, it seems, out of desire but as an act of rescue. "We walked through the wet grass to the great misty oaks," she says, "as if somebody was calling us for help there." Remembering that this act of rescue is exactly what Blanche, Alma, and Brick failed to perform, we realize that Williams means us to accept Catharine as entirely good. Although Sebastian is the loveless rejector who is punished for his sins, there is a surprising similarity between his vision of a world dominated by remorseless cruelty—as expressed in the description of the Encantadas, the Galápagos Islands, where baby sea turtles are killed and devoured by carnivorous birds of prey—and the vision of a world undergoing perpetual punishment expressed in "Desire and the Black Masseur." However, in punishing Sebastian, Williams is not disclaiming this vision. Sebastian's sin lay not in perceiving the world as, in Williams's darkest vision, it is, but in his believing, with a pride bordering on hubris, that he could exalt himself above his kind, could feed upon people like one of the devouring birds of the Encantadas. But as Sebastian had cruelly watched the turtles being eaten and fed the fruit flies to the devouring plant, so he is fed to the band of children whom he has perverted and is devoured by them.

Sebastian's crime, then, is the very one committed by Blanche, Alma, and Brick—turning away from suffering fellow creatures and offering hate instead of love. And yet there is a difficulty for the spectator in accepting the nature of Sebastian's punishment. It is not merely that Sebastian's fate is so grotesque but that, unlike Blanche and Brick, he has not performed a specific act that brings his punishment upon him; he is punished as much for what he is as for what he does. He is not only a rejector but also a homosexual, always in Williams's work an object simultaneously of sympathy and of revulsion. In the intimate connection between the guilty rejector and the martyred homosexual, the punishment visited on the former often echoes the fate of the latter, so that the two characters are not always distinguishable. In *Streetcar* the rejector and the homosexual victim were separate, but both met desperate ends. In the ambiguous Brick these figures began to converge, and in *Suddenly Last Summer* they have completely coalesced.

They remained linked in *Kingdom of Earth*—called the *Seven Descents of Myrtle* in its New York acting version—in which the sickly and effeminate Lot Ravenstock (whose elegantly sinister southern name skirts perilously close to that of Gaylord Ravenal) attempts, in a futile denial of life, to keep his property from falling into the hands of Chicken, his virile half brother (that Chicken is half black and that his domain is a rough kitchen are evident signs of an irresistible earthiness) through his unconsummated marriage to an amiable hysteric named Myrtle. As the procreative flood sweeps over the farm, however, Chicken easily takes over wife and land while Lot expires of tuberculosis after dressing himself in the clothes of his adored mother. Although Chicken is a mere caricature of virility (". . . what's able to happen between a man and a woman, just that thing, nothing more, is perfect"), Lot, the despairing transvestite, reveals a certain complexity, for he is at once shelter-seeking victim and cruel life-denier.

Once again we see the ambiguity in the vision of corruption pervading so much of Williams's work. Not only is retribution visited on the rejector of the homosexual victim, but in certain plays the homosexual himself—sterile and guilty—must be punished as well. Again and again in Williams's plays those to whom he most wishes to offer refuge and to perceive as innocent are ultimately denied their world of safety and adjudged guilty. A group of Williams's plays—*Camino Real, Orpheus Descending*, and *Sweet Bird of Youth*—develops this vision of pervasive corruption through the story of a wanderer, usually only dubiously innocent, who while searching for shelter enters a world of blatant evil and is destroyed by it.

Williams has said flatly that the sinister fantasy world of *Camino Real* "is nothing more nor less than my conception of the time and world that I live in." It is a time in which greed and brutality are the ruling forces and a world in which those pathetic souls who attempt to show some affection for their fellow creatures are remorselessly crushed and then thrown into a barrel and carted away by the street cleaners. Although this is admittedly a nightmare world, it does not differ in any essential way from the American

South as it appears in *Orpheus Descending* and *Sweet Bird of Youth* where greed, brutality, and sterility rule and where those who love are castrated or burned alive. As an epigraph to *Camino Real*, Williams has selected the opening lines of Dante's *Inferno;* the setting of the play is the world to which Orpheus descended.

As we would expect, the ruler of hell is Death; more specifically, he is the god of sterility. In *Camino Real*, Gutman, the proprietor of the Siete Mares hotel, is cruel and sinister enough, but he always remains a little remote from what happens on stage. Like Gutman, Jabe Torrance, the proprietor of the mercantile store in *Orpheus Descending*, takes little direct part in the action, but he is a far more heavily drawn figure and a far more violent antagonist. The evil creature who destroys life wherever he can find it is, as Williams describes him in a stage direction, "death's self and malignancy." He is not only "death's self" but the personification of sterility and impotence. Nurse Porter, who seems to have supernatural perception, can tell at a glance that Lady is pregnant and that Jabe is not the father. As he had burned the wine garden of Lady's father where the fig tree blossomed and true lovers met, so he calls upon the fires of the hell of impotence to burn her and her lover. (It should be noted that whereas Williams's work has changed in tone from the gentleness of *You Touched Me*, where the impotent clergyman was a figure of fun, it has not shifted in point of view.) Even more heavily than Jabe, however, Boss Finley of *Sweet Bird of Youth* is drawn as the symbol of malignant impotence. Miss Lucy, his mistress, has scrawled in lipstick across the ladies' room mirror, "Boss Finley is too old to cut the mustard." By implication, at least, he had presided over the castration of an innocent black and, as the play ends, is about to preside over that of its hero, Chance Wayne.

When Boss Finley's impotence is contrasted with Chance's attitude toward the emasculation of the black, the natures of the opposing forces in the play become clear. "You know what that is, don't you?" Chance cries. "Sex-envy is what that is, and the revenge for sex-envy which is a widespread disease that I have run into personally too often for me to doubt its existence or any manifestation." Boss Finley, Chance says, "was just called down from the hills to preach hate. I was born here to make love." Each of the three wanderers, Kilroy, Val, and Chance, had been born to make love, but each has been wounded by a hostile world. Kilroy's heart condition prevents him from continuing as a prizefighter or from staying with his "real true woman." Of the three he is the only true innocent and, significantly, the only one who is alone. Val and Chance both speak of the corrupt lives they have lived and of the waning of their youth, but in reality each is bound, not by time or by his past, but by his relationship with an older woman.

If the suggestion of homosexuality that underlies the relationship between the older woman and the younger man in Williams's novella, *The Roman Spring of Mrs. Stone*, is extended to *Orpheus* and *Sweet Bird* (in each case the ostensible woman is an older person having a forbidden affair with a beautiful young man), these works fit very easily into the pattern of ambiguity in the "punishment" group. From one point of view, the wandering love-giver—Val, whose phallic guitar is an obvious symbol, and Chance, proclaiming his vocation as lovemaker—enters the nightmare world of Hades in *Orpheus* and of what the Princess in *Sweet Bird* calls "the ogre's country at the top of the beanstalk." In the innocent attempt to rescue a lover he is brutally destroyed by the giant. (Since "Jack and the Beanstalk" is a classic oedipal fantasy, in which a boy destroys a father symbol and thereafter possesses his mother undisturbed, the imagery here has an extra level of appropriateness.) In a special variation on the wanderer material, *The Milk Train Doesn't Stop Here Anymore*, the beautiful young man comes to a ruthless but vital older woman not to rescue her through love but to preside benignly over her death.

From another point of view, however, the wanderer is not innocent but corrupt. Beneath the apparent heterosexual relationship lies one that is homosexual (the "eccentric" were among Chance's lovers; Val has "lived in corruption"), and from it spreads an aura of guilt that pervades the plays. Chance, who calculates his age by the level of rot in him, and Val, who has been "on a party" in the bars of New Orleans since he was fifteen, are trying vainly to flee from their pasts and find the sheltered realm that Williams's corrupted innocents always seek. But as before, the seeming innocent is found to be guilty and must be hideously punished. Once his moral sense has been appeased, however, Williams can allow himself the luxury of a sentimental apotheosis. *Orpheus* and *Sweet Bird* take place at Easter, and in both plays there is a suggestion that the dead wanderers should be viewed as martyred Christ figures whose spirits are resurrected respectively, in Carol Cutrere and the Princess. (Whereas the suggestion that Val Xavier does indeed have something of the savior about him is not entirely incredible, the idea that the pathetic gigolo of *Sweet Bird* could be a Christlike martyr is merely grotesque, as is the notion that Christopher—also significantly named—in *Milktrain* could be an "Angel of Death" who would "mean God" to the dying Mrs. Goforth.) Yet, whatever the wanderer's ultimate state as an object of reverence, he is allowed to reach that exalted condition only after he has been destroyed.

The absence of this conflict between the need to condemn and the desire to pardon is what distinguishes Williams's later plays and what, more than anything else, accounts for their weaknesses. Several of them—*In the Bar of a Tokyo Hotel*, *Small Craft Warnings*, and *Out Cry*—are indeed rambling discourses with little or no sense of movement toward a climax. Moreover, both in *The Mutilated* and *Gnädiges Fräulein* Williams attempts to use elements of the absurdist style, for which he has no essential affinity. But these miscalculations in technique and style are merely symptoms of an underlying problem. For whatever reason, in these plays Williams has ceased to project the opposing elements of his consciousness outward into self-sustaining dramatic entities, characters who stand in conflict with each other and upon whom Williams exercises his ambiguous judgment of innocence or guilt. Now all are innocent. All significant characters are pathetic victims—of time, of their own passions, of immutable circumstances—and all receive the playwright's sympathy in unbounded measure. But since these characters are so recognizably close to Williams and his concerns, the pity extended to them is ultimately self-pity, an emotion of very limited dramatic appeal.

The most obviously personal, and even self-indulgent, of these late plays is *Out Cry*, in which a brother and sister (suggestive of the figures in *The Glass Menagerie*), the leaders of a traveling acting company, find themselves immured alone in a mysterious foreign theater. There—on a stage dominated by a terrifying black statue, the symbol of their psychic torments—they act out a play about a brother and sister immured alone in a house dominated by ghosts of a past domestic tragedy. Unfortunately, the Pirandellesque element of the play within the play is handled without sufficient theatrical flair, and the obsessive concern with finding a private world sheltered from the assaults of external reality finally becomes stultifying. Even less appealing is the distracted artist of *In the Bar of a Tokyo Hotel*, whose madness makes him the easy victim of his cruelly vital wife, herself a victim of passing time. This contrast between inert pathos and comparative vitality, regularly presented through pairs of women in the later works (Celeste and Trinket in *The Mutilated*, the Molly-Polly figures and the Fräulein in *Gnädiges Fräulein*, Leona and Violet in *Small Craft Warnings*), runs through Williams's other plays of the late 1960s and early 1970s. But whereas this motif was handled with evocative complexity in Williams's earlier work (Amanda and Laura, Stanley and Blanche, Maggie and Brick are the most obvious examples), here everything is awash in a flood of sentimentality that invites, though it cannot induce, total sympathy for the suffering victims.

Williams's best work derives its force from the strength of his moral temper, which leads him to censure even what he most wishes to exalt. He remains committed to his romantic, neo-Lawrentian view, that the natural equals the good, that the natural instincts welling up out of the subconscious depths—and particularly the sexual instinct, whatever form it may take—

are to be trusted absolutely. But in his earlier work Williams was far too strong a moralist, far too permeated with a sense of sin, to accept such an idea with equanimity. However pathetic he made the martyred homosexual, however seemingly innocent the wandering love-giver, the moral strength that made him punish the guilty Blanche also impelled him to condemn Brick and Chance. Because he was judging the self as guilty when he most wished to believe it was innocent, because he was condemning where he most wished to offer a sheltering absolution, in order to condemn at all he sometimes had to do so with ferocious violence.

This violence, however grotesque, was never in itself the real problem in Williams's work. Nor were the disguises, transpositions, even evasions in his handling of the theme of homosexuality. They were, in fact, arguably a source of his strength, for they protected him from oversimplifications and encouraged the genuine complexity of his moral attitude to assume symbolic form in his plays. Williams's problem, then, is not that he dealt obliquely with homosexuality (the oblique view, after all, often reveals what is invisible when the object is contemplated directly) but that, especially of late but to some degree from the first, he sentimentalized. One of the central dangers confronting a romantic writer is that his commitment to the idea of the natural innocence of the self will lead him not only to see this quality as inherent in the child or man in a state of nature (Kowalski is a curious late variant on the Noble Savage) but to affirm its existence in characters who have lived all too fully in the fallen world of mortal corruption. When this easy sympathy is extended without qualification, Williams's work slips over the edge of control into the maudlin just as it slips over the opposite edge into hysteria when the opposing impulse to punish the self is dominant. When these conflicting impulses are held in some degree of balance, Williams renders perceptive judgments on his characters; then he is a moralist of some force, a playwright of some distinction.

GILBERT DEBUSSCHER

"Minting Their Separate Wills": Tennessee Williams and Hart Crane

Although unusually talkative and candid about his private life, Tennessee Williams was always comparatively reticent about his work. In fact he expressed strong feelings about the need for secrecy in order to protect "a thing that depends on seclusion till its completion for its safety." Those who expected his *Memoirs* of 1975 to shed light on his writing were therefore disappointed. However, he alluded repeatedly over the years to other writers who had deeply influenced him. When pressed for names he never failed to mention Hart Crane, D. H. Lawrence, and Anton Chekhov.

The influence of Lawrence and Chekhov has been examined extensively, but that of Hart Crane has been largely neglected by critics. This essay deals first with the indisputable traces of influence: the biographical evidence; the "presence" of Crane in titles, mottoes, and allusions; the note Williams wrote in 1965 for the slipcover of his recording of Crane's poems. Second, it develops a case suggesting that *The Glass Menagerie*, traditionally considered predominantly autobiographical, owes more to Crane than hitherto suspected. Last, an analysis of the one-act *Steps Must Be Gentle* provides new perspectives on the influence of Crane in *Suddenly Last Summer*.

I

The evidence of Crane's importance to Williams is overwhelming. First introduced to the slim volume of Crane's *Collected Poems* by Clark Mills

From *Modern Drama* 26, no. 4 (December 1983). © 1983 by the University of Toronto, Graduate Centre for the Study of Drama.

McBurney, a poet whom he had befriended in St. Louis in 1935, Williams himself acknowledged his debt in 1944 in the "Frivolous Version" of his "Preface to My Poems": "It was Clark who warned me of the existence of people like Hart Crane and Rimbaud and Rilke, and my deep and sustained admiration for Clark's writing gently but firmly removed my attention from the more obvious to the purer voices in poetry. About this time I acquired my copy of Hart Crane's collected poems which I began to read with gradual comprehension."

In this early mention Williams already reserved a special place for Crane, associating him—as he will throughout his career—with "the purer voices in poetry." "Acquired" was, however, a euphemism. In reality Williams had pilfered the copy from the library of Washington University in St. Louis, because it did not, in his opinion, get the readership it deserved. In the "Serious Version" of the same "Preface" that single book is presented as Williams's whole permanent library: "Symbolically I found a lot of books inconvenient to carry with me and gradually they dropped along the way— till finally there was only one volume with me, the book of Hart Crane. I have it with me today, my only library and all of it." And he says further: ". . . I am inclined to value Crane a little above Eliot or anyone else because of his organic purity and sheer breathtaking power. I feel that he stands with Keats and Shakespeare and Whitman."

Shortly after coming into possession of the *Poems*, Williams further "acquired" a portrait of his favorite poet from a book in the Jacksonville Public Library. He had it framed and took it with him, along with the poems, wherever his bohemian career led him. Out of the sixteen allusions to Crane in the *Letters to Donald Windham*, three are to that treasured portrait.

In addition to these two tangible reminders of Crane in Williams's surroundings, clear traces of the poet's presence can be found in the plays. In *You Touched Me*, the dramatization of a D. H. Lawrence story which Williams wrote in collaboration with Donald Windham in the early forties, there is already a passing reference to Crane. When Hadrian reads at random from Matilda's book of verse, he comes across the lines "How like a caravan my heart—Across the desert moved towards yours!," and he wonders "To-wards whose? Who is this H. C. it's dedicated to?"; Matilda shyly replies "Hart Crane. An American poet who died ten years ago." Besides the explicit reference, the two lines read by Hadrian recall the "speechless caravan" in the fifth stanza of "To Brooklyn Bridge," the piece with which Crane's epic of America opens.

The motto of *A Streetcar Named Desire* (1947) comes from the fifth stanza of Crane's "The Broken Tower," a poetic farewell and a densely compressed account of his own career, completed barely a month before his suicide in the Caribbean near Florida:

> And so it was I entered the broken world
> To trace the visionary company of love, its voice
> An instant in the wind (I know not whither hurled)
> But not for long to hold each desperate choice.

These four lines describe Blanche DuBois's dramatic march to oblivion which began with her fateful entrance into the Vieux Carré. They reveal the playwright's conception of not one, but two "broken world[s]": that of faded illusions (the crumbled plantation in the past), and that of disheartening reality (the dingy apartment of the present); "one gone with the wind, the other barely worth having."

This motto, then, introduces the first of the strong polarities from which the play derives much of its tension. It reveals in the playwright an attitude of deliberateness and detachment from the material of his plays with which Williams is rarely credited by his commentators. The motto signals that, since both Belle Reve and Elysian Fields are stamped as "broken world[s]," and since life is defined as the making of "desperate choice[s]," the existential itineraries of both Stanley and Blanche—not of one to the exclusion of the other—lead to final disaster. It is a measure of the playwright's artistic control that the balance—or ambiguity—introduced by the preliminary warning of the motto is maintained to the very end of the play.

In the following year, 1948, Williams published *Summer and Smoke*. This title comes from Crane's "Emblems of Conduct." The alliterative phrase appears in the only two lines—the first two of the three quoted below—that are Crane's own, inserted between fragments gleaned from the then unpublished manuscripts of Samuel Greenberg:

> By that time summer and smoke were past.
> Dolphins still played, arching the horizons,
> But only to build memories of spiritual gates.

The peaceful autumnal image sums up the general mood of the poem, "a sadly beautiful appraisal of a world no longer animated by a genuine religious or visionary consciousness. . . ."

This title from Crane's work evokes the nostalgia of a world long past its apogee and now declining. Williams's clear intent is further reinforced in the only passage where Crane's phrase is echoed, when Alma describes her former "Puritan" self (and by inference all those who lived by this code), late in the play, as having "died last summer—suffocated in smoke from something on fire inside her."

To those who perceive this variation of the title words and are aware of the nostalgic message of Crane's poem, Williams is suggesting through Alma that the South and its traditional way of life have collapsed under the burden of a code of morals emphasizing spiritual values and repressing the claims of man's physical nature. The title is, in fact, Williams's poetic statement of his theme of fading civilization and the disappearance of the Old South, a theme which is to be found not only here, but also in *The Glass Menagerie* and *A Streetcar Named Desire*.

Although Williams's letters mention Crane in following years as often as before, it is only in 1959, with the publication of *Sweet Bird of Youth*, that Crane regains his former prominence in the plays. The motto here comes from Crane's *White Buildings* collection, where it appears in a piece entitled "Legend":

> Relentless caper for all those who step
> The legend of their youth into the noon.

These two lines are pressed into service by Williams as a warning. R. W. B. Lewis describes the poem: "It was as one who had learned the danger of moral despair and who had embodied the lesson in song that Crane offered his example to the young: as a 'relentless caper'—a playfully serious and morally unrelenting and impenitent model—for those who will in turn move through youthful experience toward maturity. Crane presents his own life as allegory to those who have yet to live theirs."

The selection by Williams of this particular passage introduces one of the play's main motifs, the attaining of maturity and the danger of trying to extend the ideal fiction of youth, its "legend," into the heart of middle age. It thus establishes Williams's definitely moralistic intentions. Like Crane's poem, his play relates an experience which instructs us about the nature of good and evil, and from which rules can be deduced to govern the conduct of life. The dramatic itinerary of the characters, their "[r]elentless caper," is presented as a warning; their "legend," in both meanings of "key" and "exemplary life," is meant to convey a message of moral import. Chance's final speech about recognizing "the enemy, Time, in us all," however clumsily tacked on, confirms the seemingly paradoxical ambition of *Sweet Bird of Youth* to be a modern morality play, as implicitly announced in the motto from Crane.

Whether they appear as motto or title, the lines from Crane are important, less as reminders of the poems from which they are lifted, than for their intrinsic meanings which provide a particular viewpoint on the material, a perspective suggested by the author on the play's events and characters. Because they constitute a standard by which the play must be measured, they are an integral and indispensable part of it.

In 1962, in *The Night of the Iguana*, Williams again alludes to Crane. A reference to the portrait of Crane painted by the Mexican artist David Siqueiros in 1931 appears in the dialogue between Shannon and Hannah, a painter who is also the play's amateur psychoanalyst. She is trying to sketch a picture not so much of Shannon's outward appearance as of a deeper reality hidden within him:

> HANNAH: . . . You're a very difficult subject. When the
>   Mexican painter Siqueiros did his portrait of the American
>   poet Hart Crane he had to paint him with closed eyes
>   because he couldn't paint his eyes open—there was too
>   much suffering in them and he couldn't paint it.
> SHANNON: Sorry, but I'm not going to close my eyes for you.
>   I'm hypnotizing myself—at least trying to—by looking at
>   the light on the orange tree . . . leaves.
> HANNAH: That's all right. I can paint your eyes open.

The reference constitutes an invitation to compare Shannon and Crane, but the lady's curt remark firmly establishes the discrepancy between her subject and that of Siqueiros. Shannon's self-indulgent histrionics are deflated by this deliberate comparison with the suffering experienced by Crane and registered in the painting. Like the submerged contrast between Shannon and his patron, St. Lawrence, the allusion to Crane reveals the blend of compassionate understanding and irony with which Williams regards his character.

Williams's continued preoccupation with the poet culminated in 1965, when he agreed to read a selection of poems by Crane for Caedmon Records and to provide a note for the slipcover. In the note Williams reveals his familiarity with the facts of Crane's life and mentions two early scholarly works devoted to the poet: the "superb" biography written by Philip Horton (1937), and the "marvelous" collection of letters edited by Brom Weber (1952). The particular incidents on which Williams concentrates are illustrations of themes and motifs basic to his own creative work. He focuses with characteristic dramatic flair on the most intense moments of Crane's life, the day of his suicide and the emotionally charged night immediately preceding it. Of the latter we are told that Crane "had visited the sailors' quarters and the visit had turned out badly. They had treated him mockingly and violently." Regarding the day itself, Williams describes how Peggy Cowley, the woman with whom Crane was traveling back to the United States, "had . . . suffered, that same night before, the pointless accident of a book of matches blowing up in her hand and burning her hand severely. She was not in a state to sympathize much with her friend, and so what happened happened."

Crane's confrontation with the outside world is presented here as similar to that of many of the more sensitive characters in Williams's work, particularly the artists and poets. Wherever they turn in their search for understanding or togetherness, in their quest for "the visionary company of love," they meet with rejection, hostility, or indifference. The slipcover note further mentions the writing block Crane experienced in the last two years of his life, after adverse criticism of *The Bridge* had reawakened self-doubt:

> Crane had lived and worked with such fearful intensity—and without fearful intensity Crane was unable to work at all—that his nerves were exhausted and for many months he had been able to produce only one important poem, *The Broken Tower*, a poem that contains these beautiful and ominous lines:
>
> *The bells, I say, the bells*
> *Break down their tower.*

"By the bells breaking down their tower," Williams goes on to say, Crane "undoubtedly meant the romantic and lyric intensity of his vocation." That Williams considers the lines "ominous" indicates that he views the creative process here, as elsewhere in his own work, as a consuming experience. The production of poetry, and more generally of art, leaves the artist ultimately exhausted, spent as a runner and broken in body.

One cannot help noting the parallel with Williams's own career, which went into a prolonged eclipse in the early 1960s—at the time he recorded the Crane poems—when he doggedly rewrote *The Milk Train Doesn't Stop Here Anymore*, and relied more and more heavily on alcohol and drugs to alleviate doubts about his artistic future. His remarks about Crane's state of mind could therefore apply equally to himself: "He lived in a constant inner turmoil and storm that liquor, which he drank recklessly, was no longer able to quieten, to hold in check."

Finally, the Caedmon note contains a quotation whose gloss points to one of the fascinations Crane's life held for Williams. The short passage from

"For the Marriage of Faustus and Helen" (erroneously identified by Williams as belonging to "The Broken Tower") reads: "There is the world dimensional for those untwisted by the love of things irreconcilable." Williams interprets these lines as follows: "[T]he meaning . . . is more open to varying interpretations. Could he have meant that his vocation as a poet of extraordinary purity, as well as intensity, was hopelessly at odds with his night-time search for love in water-front bars?" The homosexual Williams of the *Memoirs* is here clearly identifying with that facet of Crane's personality which he detects in the cryptic lines.

Although obviously devoted to Crane, the record note reveals, beyond the sketched portrait of the poet, a figure that is modeled after Williams himself and all the poet-characters in whom he had projected himself up to 1965. It strongly suggests, further, that if Crane enduringly captured Williams's imagination, the cause was biographical as well as poetic. Williams was aware, as he later stated in an interview with Cecil Brown, of the truly stunning similarity of his and Crane's formative years, family situations, and aspirations. Crane's small-town origins; his family life, torn between egotistical parents who turned him into the battlefield of their marital strife; his fervent attachment to both his neurotic mother (with whom he was later to fall out) and his indulgent, doting grandmother; his early aversion to and later reconciliation with a father who opposed his aspirations as a poet and insisted that he enter the family business; the bohemian wanderlust that prevented him from settling down permanently; his bouts of ill health which were often psychosomatic in origin; and finally his uphill fight for artistic integrity in an uncomprehending world, his torment by spells of self-doubt and despair that led him to suicide—all of these conditions, together with a sexuality unfocused but predominantly homoerotic, were traits of Crane's life and personality in which Williams must have recognized himself as in a mirror. I submit, therefore, that Hart Crane contributed forcefully to Williams's perception of himself as revealed by the semiautobiographical characters who populate his plays: the figure of the wandering poet, the doomed artist who haunts the published work, appearing as early as *Battle of Angels* (1938); a figure who finds his most surprising incarnations in Tom Wingfield in *The Glass Menagerie* (1944) and Sebastian Venable in *Suddenly Last Summer* (1958).

II

The Glass Menagerie belongs to the period of Williams's greatest involvement with the poetry of Hart Crane, a time when the playwright quotes from Crane repeatedly both in the correspondence with Donald Windham and in the plays. Although at first sight Crane appears to be totally absent from this particular play, in fact it is only the mode of Crane's "presence" in *The Glass Menagerie* which is different. Whereas in *A Streetcar Named Desire* and *Summer and Smoke* he is emphatically visible through motto or title, in this case he pervades the texture of the play without being explicitly mentioned.

There is nevertheless one objective clue (perhaps there are even two, as I shall point out) that attests to Williams's use of Crane. In scene six, Amanda appears in her "resurrected" yellow dress for the "jonquil scene," a moment of great intensity whose special quality Williams describes in the stage direction: *"the legend of her youth is nearly revived."* One recalls again the passage from Crane's poem "Legend" which was to serve as motto for *Sweet Bird of Youth*. This stage direction is a clear hint for the reader and the director aware of the Crane-Williams crosscurrents that Amanda, in her pathetic attempt to recapture her past glory, is to experience the disillusionment of those who force themselves into a "[r]elentless caper," ceaselessly reliving their pasts. The borrowing further confirms that the southern background recollected by Amanda is actually a "legend," that is, both a key to understanding her character and motivations, and a story, a fable, even perhaps a lie. It suggests that the past was never as idyllic as she would like to remember it, but at the same time—to those who are aware of Crane's poem, and beyond it, of John Donne's "The Canonization"—it indicates that this is a cautionary tale for all those who must turn their backs on their youthful pasts and move forward to maturity and decline. The borrowing relegated to a stage direction is a muted reminder at this crucial moment that Amanda's fate is intended as a model, a "legend" for consideration and enlightenment.

A more cryptic reminder of Crane may be found later in the same scene, again in a stage direction. In the course of a conversation with Jim, Tom rhapsodically describes a future that involves neither his mother and sister, nor the shoe factory. As the image of "the sailing vessel with the Jolly Roger again" is projected on a screen in the background, Tom leans over the rail of the fire escape on which he stands, which has now become the rail of an imaginary ocean liner, and the stage direction reads: *"He looks like a voyager."* Williams's use of "voyager" cannot fail, for someone familiar (as the playwright was) with the Crane canon, to evoke the "Voyages" poems. Indeed the word so fittingly limns Hart Crane that John Unterecker entitled his monumental 1969 biography of the poet *Voyager: A Life of Hart Crane*.

The short scene in which Tom leans on the rail may be, then, a dramatic reconstruction of the last minutes of the poet's life before he escaped, as

Tom is planning to do, from a world that had become too oppressive to bear. What we may have, therefore, is a shadowy portrait in Tom Wingfield of Hart Crane himself, at a most critical moment of his life. Just as Williams's own face could be glimpsed behind his portrait of Crane in the record note, so the figure of Crane shows through Tom Wingfield's portrait in *The Glass Menagerie*, providing it with tantalizing shadows.

Moreover, although there is by now a long tradition, supported by declarations of the playwright himself, that the figure of Amanda Wingfield is a portrait of Williams's own mother, one could make a convincing case for Grace Hart Crane, the poet's mother, as the model for some aspects of the high-strung, possessive Amanda. One should recall, in this connection, the anecdote of Mrs. Williams's visit to Chicago for a performance of *The Glass Menagerie*, at the end of which she was appalled to hear that Laurette Taylor might have considered her the real-life model for the character she portrayed in the play. Furthermore, a growing number of commentators have noticed, again following the playwright's indications, that the play is hardly a faithful picture of the Williamses' circumstances around 1935/1936, and that the three characters supposedly modeled on the author and his family have all undergone important changes in the process of dramatization.

If one remembers the picture of Crane's mother as it emerges from the accounts of Philip Horton and John Unterecker, however, one realizes not only that the relationships of the sons with their respective mothers are comparable, but also that the two women show a remarkable degree of resemblance even in details. For example, Mrs. Crane, suddenly deprived of the financial security that had thus far seemed assured, contemplated taking a job as "hostess in a restaurant perhaps, assistant in one of the city's hotels, anything that would let her draw on the only assets she had, her charm and her beauty." Of this situation more than an echo can be found in the job Amanda actually holds (she being a more practical-minded woman) "at Famous-Barr . . . demonstrating those . . . *(She indicates a brassiere with her hands)*". In Williams's conception the job—which his own mother never had to envisage—capitalized on Amanda's physical appeal; one of the early drafts sent to Audrey Wood reads: "(Amanda has been working as a model for a matron's dresses at downtown depart. store and has just lost the job because of faded appearance)."

The picture of Mrs. Crane painted by Unterecker in the following paragraph is exactly like that of Amanda, with her reminiscences about the carefree Blue Mountain girl courted by seventeen gentlemen callers: "As she and Hart would talk through her problems, both of them would look back fondly to Hart's childhood, to the days when financial security seemed limitless—the good times of gardeners, maids, cooks, chauffeurs, handymen, tutors—until, magnifying the past out of all proportion,they would make the present unbearable."

These glimpses of Grace Crane cohere into a prototype for Amanda as plausible as the playwright's own mother. But the resemblance between Mrs. Crane and Amanda is never more convincing than in the following passage: "For Grace's real problem—and to a considerable extent, Hart's—was the memory of former affluence. . . . Each of them found it easier to eat badly than to dress badly. 'Keeping up appearances' was for Grace not just a casual compulsion but a life-and-death matter." Such a portrait anticipates Amanda's DAR outfit, her compulsive refurbishing of the apartment, the purchase of new clothes for Laura, her metamorphosis into a southern belle in her own "resurrected" dress, and her evocation of the past for the benefit of the bewildered Jim O'Connor.

Let me now advance a further argument: beyond these strong biographical parallels with Crane and his mother, the play also reflects the influence of Crane as a poet and, in particular, of one poem, "The Wine Menagerie," from the collection *White Buildings*. To begin with, there is the striking similarity of the titles. The present title of the play was arrived at only after various other possibilities—such as "Portrait of a Girl in Glass," "The Gentleman Caller," and "If You Breathe It Breaks or Portrait of a Girl in Glass"—had been discarded. I suggest, therefore, that only after growing aware of the correspondences between his play and Crane's poem, presumably late in the process of fashioning the final version, Williams hit upon this felicitous title for the play that was to establish his reputation throughout the world. It is my guess that at some point during the rehearsals—perhaps well into December 1944, when Eddie Dowling and George Jean Nathan "advised" him to introduce the drunk scene finally included at the beginning of scene six—Williams was reminded of "The Wine Menagerie" and used this as the spark for his final title. The first two lines of the poem could have served, in fact, as a reasonable starting frame for the whole scene:

> Invariably when the wine redeems the sight
> Narrowing the mustard scansions of the eyes.

Regarding these lines, R. W. B. Lewis comments that "[t]he consumption of much wine . . . suddenly clarified the poet's vision and greatly increased his interpretive and creative powers." Tom's drunkenness in the play is a source of similar vision, and even the "faint Eucharistic overtone" that Lewis discerns in the association of "wine" and "redeems" finds a parallel—though perhaps a sardonic one—in the Easter symbolism that pervades Tom's speech.

In his conversation with Laura, Tom presents the stage show he has just seen in terms that leave little doubt of its symbolic connection to his own fate: ". . . There was a big stage show! The headliner on this stage show was Malvolio the Magician. He performed wonderful tricks [. . .] But the wonderfullest trick of all was the coffin trick. We nailed him into a coffin and he got out of the coffin without removing one nail [. . .] There is a trick that would come in handy for me—get me out of this two-by-four situation!" Through Tom's report we come to realize that escaping the social and emotional web in which he is entangled without hurting anyone and hence without feeling guilty is a trick that only a magician could bring off. This truth revealed in drunkenness helps justify Tom's final action in the play; it helps make the audience accept the fact that "to escape from a trap he has to act without pity."

The second stanza of the poem introduces the idea that the whole should be seen as the intoxicated musing—"a sort of boozy approximation of direct statement"—of the poet, who also figures as a character in the bar scene which the lines evoke. This double role of writer and protagonist is paralleled in the play, where Tom is both the narrator and a character in the story he tells. Moreover, several Crane commentators have noticed that—like the play—"The Wine Menagerie" supports a reading in terms of the poet's biography. And there are further similarities: Crane's poem suggests, as Sherman Paul has emphasized, that "[t]he man and woman, whose combat [the narrator-actor] witnesses . . . are father and mother seen from the 'distance' of childhood." This is essentially the point of view of Tom, whose "distance in time" provides him with a perspective akin to, although not identical with, that of the poet in Crane's work. The seasonal setting and atmosphere of the two works present additional affinities. The bleak early winter landscape of the poem, which contributes to the Eliotian atmosphere of the whole, is traceable also in the general mood of the play. It informs the urban setting common to play and poem, and presides over the play's description of the "[c]ouples . . . [in] the alley . . . kissing behind ash pits and telephone poles," who could have been lifted by Williams from the context Crane had earlier devised for them.

Thematically, too, the poem offers a basis for comparison with the play. Uncharacteristically for Crane, "[l]oss is the primary emotion the poem reaches into. . . . " Now "loss" is a key concept in Williams's vision, a feeling that he finds inseparable from the human condition. "[T]he monosyllable of the clock is Loss, loss, loss, unless you devote your heart to its opposition," he has said. Surveying the isolation of the derelict "menagerie" assembled in the bar, Crane's poem ends in sadness, or—as Paul has aptly put it—on "a low plateau of resolve." This again is a perfect description of the final moment of *The Glass Menagerie*. The mood of melancholy and nostalgia suffusing the play may therefore owe as much to Hart Crane as to Anton Chekhov, who has long been thought its primary source.

The nostalgia at the end of the play is poignantly enhanced by Tom's ultimate departure, by his painful act of tearing himself away from his family and the guilt associated with this emotional and physical exile. Tom's basic motivation—a determination to be true to his own self—and his final summoning up of courage are clearly foreshadowed in the poem, where the young man is exhorted to:

> Rise from the dates and crumbs. And walk away. . . .
>
> . . . .
> Beyond the wall. . . .
> . . . .
> And fold your exile on your back again.

Both characters come in the end to accept, not without second thoughts, that freedom and its corollary, loneliness, are essential to the activity which they see as their fundamental reason to live.

The situation of Tom in the epilogue may have been suggested by that of the speaker in the poem, a solitary man in a bar looking at a display of multicolored bottles which reflect the movements and attitudes of patrons, images encompassing the past as much as the present. Peering in drunken fascination at the changing surfaces of the "glozening decanters," the poet manages to focus on essentials, "[n]arrowing the mustard scansions of the eyes." He thus sees through or beyond the chaotic reality that otherwise claims his attention, and through vision he imposes an order on it, "asserts a vision in the slumbering gaze."

Tom looks not at bottles on display in a bar, but at delicately colored vials in the window of a perfume shop. The vials too present an informal, unpatterned reality, "like bits of a shattered rainbow." They reflect, far beyond the drab winter of the city, the past of Tom's family life, "conscript[ing]" him (to use Crane's word) to the shadowy glow of the menagerie. In Williams's case, the play itself is the vision that imposes order and exorcises—if only temporarily—the conflicting feelings of relief and guilt stirred in Tom by memory.

Finally, poem and play have a further point of confluence. Crane's poem establishes a number of mythic parallels for its central incident, a confrontation between a man and a woman in a bar. Evoking the violent meetings of Judith and Holofernes, Salome and John the Baptist, and Petrushka and his "valentine," it presents the experience as one of dismemberment and decapitation. The figurine central to the glass collection, the unicorn, undergoes a comparable mutilation when its little horn is accidentally broken off. This interpretation is particularly apt if one recalls that the glass animal represents Rose, the playwright's sister, and that the loss of the horn is probably an attenuated echo of her prefrontal lobotomy—a modern surgical version of decapitation—which alleviated her schizophrenia but left her maimed for life.

Both poem and play can rightfully be seen, then, as "an actual incident, in a clear setting, with visible characters, and progressing from a meandering meditation to a moment of clear decision—a decision, needless to say, about the exercise of the poet's visionary power and touching upon his creative resolve." Rather than being considered an indulgent wallowing in sentimental reminiscences, *The Glass Menagerie* may be viewed through a Cranean glass as a dramatic statement about the artist and his predicament. This perspective may lead to a further conclusion, again constituting a warning for all who would limit the play to a faithful account of Williams's early days in St. Louis, that *The Glass Menagerie* is as much literature as confession, as much imaginative reading as autobiography, as much Crane as Williams.

III

The publication in 1980 of a short play entitled *Steps Must Be Gentle* shed new light not only on Williams's familiarity with the facts of Crane's biography, but also on the pervasive influence of Crane, both as man and poet, on Williams's writing and particularly on the play *Suddenly Last Summer*. Specifically described in the subtitle as "A Dramatic Reading for Two Performers," *Steps Must Be Gentle* presents an imaginary dialogue between Hart Crane and his mother. Although the play takes place in an unspecified location, sea sounds constantly remind us that the poet is speaking from the bottom of the ocean, presumably immediately after Grace Hart Crane's death on July 30, 1947. There is virtually no plot. The tenuous "connection" is interrupted several times, threatened with extinction; sentences are left unfinished, and Hart feigns to misunderstand or not to hear what his mother is so eager to tell him.

The short piece concentrates entirely on the reproachful reminiscences of the protagonists. Grace cannot, even after death, forgive her son for his four-year-long silence. Hart, who wants nothing more than to be left in peace at the bottom of the ocean, remembers in icy tones how both his parents turned him into a human misfit, how his father made him beg for the little money he doled out to him, and his mother, for recognition of the sexual deviancy he had confessed to her. Grace counters by pointing out that the last fifteen years of her life were devoted to preserving and enhancing Hart's posthumous reputation, to gathering the poetry that she now considers, over his protestations, as much hers as his. From the outset she appears to be on the verge of telling her son how she managed to survive without friends or money, dedicating herself totally to this work of love. When his mother broaches the subject of his deviant sexuality again, Hart changes the conversation by insisting on the question of her occupation, and she finally reveals, "I've been employed at nights as a scrubwoman, Hart."

The revelation of the degrading of his once beautiful and elegant mother profoundly upsets the dead poet; his jealously preserved rest is disturbed forever, one assumes, since he is heard at the end of the play calling out her name "(*more and more faintly but with anguish*)" in an ironic echo of her own insistent "Hart?—Hart?—Son?" "(*repeated a number of times in various tones, from tenderly beseeching to desperately demanding*)" at the start of the play. The outcome makes it clear that Grace has reached her aim: she has broken through the willful indifference with which her son had surrounded himself. She has imposed her emotional blackmail on him; he is again, and now forever, dependent on her.

The title itself is from Crane's poem "My Grandmother's Love Letters," in the collection *White Buildings*. It expresses with painful irony the perception that to reach a balanced understanding of sorts, to bridge the distance—physical, temporal, and emotional—that separates them, Hart and Grace must proceed cautiously. "Over the greatness of such space/Steps must be gentle," the poet warns. The characters in the play are unable, however, to heed the warning implicit in the title.

At the start of their impossible conversation, Hart reminds his mother that "[i]t's been a long while since we have existed for each other," that death has severed the blood tie that once bound them together. Using a metaphor from the poem "At Melville's Tomb," where the "dice of drowned men's bones. . . . / . . . / Beat on the dusty shore," he says: "There is no blood in bones that were cast and scattered as gambler's dice on the sea's floor. This borrowing and the poem from which it comes throw an interesting light on the relationship of Williams to Melville, a relationship that might possibly involve a third presence. Although there is no doubt that Williams was acquainted firsthand with the novelist, it is equally clear that he was often reminded of Melville through Crane's direct or oblique references to him, as he states in a letter of March 25, 1946: "I was reminded of that work [*Billy Budd*] recently while reading over Crane's 'Cutty Sark.' " The quotation from Melville that we shall find in *Suddenly Last Summer* may therefore be, paradoxically, another indirect reference to Crane.

A further allusion to Crane's poetry emerges in the poet's punning reminder that " 'Sundered parentage,' Grace, is that from which I chose to descend to the sea's floor." The irony is bitter and manifold. In his evocation of "the curse of sundered parentage" in his poem "Quaker Hill," the poet is talking about personal experience, as commentators have recognized, but he transcends this immediate context to indicate symbolically the "cleavage between present and past," "the sundering of Pocahontas and Maquokeeta." In the play, however, the phrase "sundered parentage" is brought back to its literal sense, as in the verb "to descend," which refers metaphorically both to genealogical origin (" 'Sundered parentage,' Grace, is that from which I . . . descend") and to actual movement ("I chose to descend to the sea's floor"). The pun, reminiscent of Crane's verbal strategies elsewhere, thus implies a barbed reproach that his parents' marital feud and the psychic consequences it entailed for him were the curse which presided over Crane's suicide.

This reproach is followed by another, related allusion, again to stanza five of "The Broken Tower," the passage of Crane's poetry frequently mentioned by Williams. In this context the lines regain a literal meaning. After referring to his antagonistic progenitors as his "Sundered parentage," the poet naturally thinks of his birth, his "enter[ing] the broken world," a reality whose fragmentation he would seek to overcome through poetry. Grace later echoes these and earlier lines of the same poem when she reveals to Hart that she has had no occupation since his death other than the preserving of his reputation: ". . . I have carried the stones to build your tower again." The comment is fraught with poignant irony. The metaphorical tower had all too painful and unpoetic a literalness for the mother who, having contributed definitely, though perhaps unintentionally, to the fragmentation of the world of her poet-son, then devoted the last fifteen years of her miserable life as a scrubwoman to gathering material on which his posthumous fame would firmly rest.

In this play more than anywhere else in Williams's work, the elements selected from Crane's biography reveal a parallelism with the playwright's own life which could not fail to have been recognized by Williams. The contrast between an elegant, charming mother and a mercantile, obtuse father, the tortured love-hate relationship with both of them, the pathetic and painful acknowledgment of homosexuality—all of these factors must have struck a deeply responsive chord.

In 1947, *Steps Must Be Gentle* contained the seeds of what was to develop into *Suddenly Last Summer* (1958). Nancy M. Tischler has already suspected that the figure of Hart Crane may have served as a model for Sebastian Venable, but much more than a simple identification between the two poets can now be traced to Crane's biography. Central to the resemblance between *Steps Must Be Gentle* and *Suddenly Last Summer* is the motivation ascribed to the two mothers, Grace Hart Crane and Violet Venable: their determination to preserve their sons' posthumous reputations. In the early play Grace describes this ambition in words that might equally well have been spoken by Violet: "I have made it my dedication, my vocation, to protect your name, your legend, against the filthy scandals that you'd seemed determined to demolish them with. Despite my age, my illness . . . ."

In *Suddenly Last Summer* the real-life traits of Hart Crane appear splintered, divided up among three characters: first, the dead Sebastian, the homosexual author of a limited, practically unknown body of work reserved for a coterie, who travels restlessly in pursuit of "vision"; second, the "glacially brilliant" Dr. Cuckrowicz with his "icy charm," in whom both Mrs. Venable and Catharine recognize a number of Sebastian's features, and who represents an aspect of Crane seen in *Steps*, where Grace reproaches her son for his "icy language" and frigid attitude; finally, Catharine, whose uncompromising insistence on the truth threatens the Sebastian myth, and who embodies the self-destructive tendencies that led to Crane's suicide.

The tortured relationship between Hart and Grace, the pattern of a genteel but domineering mother and a submissive son, the figure of an absent, despised, or otherwise negligible father, and the use of emotional blackmail are all aspects of *Steps Must Be Gentle* clearly foreshadowing the complex bonds between Sebastian and Violet. Grace's claim that "I exist in your blood as you exist in mine—"and her appropriation of her son's poetry (" . . . I have defended your poetry with my life, because— . . . It was mine, too" postulate a complete, intimate symbiosis of mind and body between mother and son that is reflected in Violet's exultant affirmation of almost incestuous unity: "We were a famous couple. People didn't speak of Sebastian and his mother or Mrs. Venable and her son, they said 'Sebastian and Violet, Violet and Sebastian . . .' "; and in her claims that "[w]*ithout* me, [the poem was] impossible [to deliver], Doctor" or that "[h]e was *mine!*"

Further echoes of *Steps* can be found. For example, there is the memorial foundation that Mrs. Venable promises to establish for the young doctor if he agrees to cut out part of Catharine's brain: the financial equivalent of the lofty poetic tower Grace claims to have rebuilt.

The end of *Suddenly Last Summer*, in which it is revealed that Sebastian was eaten alive by the young boys, was shocking material in 1958, not only because it describes cannibalism—however metaphorically this may have been meant—but also because it blasphemously endows Sebastian with the status of a Eucharistic sacrificial victim. This characteristic blend of religious ritual and sex, a trademark of Williams's since *Battle of Angels* was foreshadowed in *Steps* in a similarly startling equation of Communion with a cannibalistic version of fellatio. Grace exclaims there: "Feed you with *what*, Hart? . . . the—sex of sailors picked up in Brooklyn, dockside bars, as if they were the thin bits of bread that symbolized Christ's flesh at Holy Communion, and their seed as if it were His—blood!"

The new perspective on the relationship between the Venables provided by the early play about the Cranes prompts me to identify the vague but definitely "tropical" locale of Sebastian's last day as Mexico, a country dear to both Crane and Williams. Further, it raises a question as to Mrs. Venable's character and actions: can we be so sure that Mrs. Venable is unaware of her son's sexual deviancy? In the most recent full-length study devoted to Williams, the author still maintains serenely that "Catharine . . . eventually realized that [Sebastian] was a homosexual and was using her to make contacts for him. He had used his mother in the same way without Mrs. Venable's realizing it. . . ." And it is true that Catharine seems to believe, perhaps genuinely, that if Mrs. Venable procured for her son, she did so "*Not consciously!* She didn't *know* that she was procuring for him in the smart, the fashionable places they used to go to before last summer!"

Yet how could Mrs. Venable have failed to see the truth, when she herself reports to Cuckrowicz: "My son, Sebastian, was chaste. Not c-h-a-s-e-d! Oh, he was chased in that way of spelling it, too, we had to be very fleet-footed I can tell you, with his looks and his charm, to keep ahead of pursuers, every kind of pursuer!" It would take a particularly obtuse character—quite unlike Mrs. Venable—not to see the light after twenty-five years of this kind of life. The new Cranean viewpoint on *Suddenly Last Summer*—notice the pun on chased-chaste—may suggest that, contrary to Catharine's belief (too readily accepted as the truth by some critics), Violet does know but cannot accept the sexual nature of her son. Her actions in the play are an attempt to hide from the outside world this unaccepted and, in her eyes, unacceptable truth. When the attempt fails, she takes refuge from that truth in death ("I won't speak again. I'll keep still, if it kills me") or in madness, as suggested by her erratic outburst at the end of the play. *Steps Must Be Gentle* and the new light it throws on *Suddenly Last Summer* allow us another glimpse of the complex artistry of the later play, further justifying, in my opinion, its reputation as one of Williams's best works.

The poet-wanderer, the romantic quester in search of purity, the non-conformist faced with hostile surroundings has haunted the world of Tennessee Williams from the beginning. And from the beginning too, commentators have been misled—not least by the playwright himself—into believing that this figure was a hardly disguised self-portrait. In retrospect, however, it appears that if the plays are to be trusted more than the playwright, they may tell a different tale and provide us with signposts that point in a new, hitherto little heeded direction.

The evidence accumulated in this essay spans Williams's entire public career from 1938 to 1980, and takes such forms as titles or mottoes; direct or submerged allusions; quotations of various lengths appearing in plays, short stories, introductions, and essays. It strongly suggests that in the process of "minting [his] separate will," of creating his character of the artist, Williams had been referring, almost systematically, not solely to his own experience, but to that of Hart Crane.

In his effort to rise from the intensely personal to the general, in his attempt to "[snatch] the eternal out of the desperately fleeting," Williams molded Hart Crane, both as a man and as a poet, into a heightened image of himself, an idealized alter ego and a tutelary power. Through Crane, Williams succeeded in "looking out, not in," in transcending his immediate self and formulating a compelling statement about the artist in the modern world.

C. W. E. BIGSBY

Valedictory

By degrees the plight of the writer and the question of the nature of reality moved to the forefront of [Tennessee Williams's] work. Following the crisis of the 1960s, referred to by Williams as his "stoned decade" because of his personal retreat to drink and narcotics—which were now no longer a metaphor for escapism but the primary mechanism for that escape—he engaged more directly issues always implicit in his work. Earlier in his career he had created characters who invented worlds, who chose to see existence through the rose-coloured light that escaped its cliché origin only because the force of its personal significance was communicated so powerfully. His characters turned their worlds into theatrical sets, consciously subverting a reality, the substantiality of which they conceded by their very defensiveness. It was by an act of will that the naturalistic world was reflected in sets which were never allowed to assert their naturalistic logic. Solid walls dissolved or disappeared into space, light was apt to soften, discordant sounds to reveal a hidden harmony under the impact of the transforming sensibility. But the real still existed. The debate was over the nature and extent of its authority.

By the time of *The Two Character Play* (1967), rewritten as *Out Cry* in 1971 and then rewritten again in 1973, he was ready to address a more directly ontological question. What was the nature of reality and how was it to be known? Since the process of human relationships and the assertion of identity were, as he now saw it, in some sense essentially theatrical, indeed

From *A Critical Introduction to Twentieth-Century American Drama 2: Tennessee Williams, Arthur Miller, Edward Albee.* © 1984 by C. W. E. Bigsby. Cambridge University Press, 1984.

since that social world which he had earlier perceived as an indistinct sense of menace was itself simply a series of socially endorsed fictions, in what sense were the individual fiction-making skills aberrant?

Out Cry is ostensibly set in a subterranean theatre in which a brother and sister, abandoned by their company and, in due course, by their audience (assuming it ever to have existed), enact a play in which they apparently play themselves. Yet as former mental patients, even their role as actors is suspect. Whatever their circumstances, they are trapped, in the play-within-the-play by a paralysing fear, and otherwise by the locked doors of the theatre. Abandoned and isolated, they retreat into performance, trying to generate a literal and metaphoric warmth, acting out their desperation, in the sense both of enacting and discharging their desperation. The line between fiction and reality dissolves, if it were indeed ever clear. Much of the scenery, we are told, has failed to arrive and, indeed, the fixed points which would enable clear distinctions to be made are equally missing. There is no location. No triangulation is possible. One of the characters announces that "my watch froze to death" and describes their present setting as "somewhere that seems like nowhere." The only reliable reality lies in the sense of abandonment, the shared plight, and the desire to create with ultimate significance. Indeed, acting and being are presented as being synonymous. It is the proof of existence. I act, therefore I exist. For Williams as for Nietzsche the ability to lie, it seems, is the source of transcendence. It is definitional.

Williams is clearly moving into the territory of Pirandello, of Stoppard's early plays and Albee's later ones. His interests here are in part those of Beckett and of Pinter (in plays such as *Old Times, No Man's Land* and *Monologue*). His sentimentality survives only in a mannered language and the self-conscious poignancy of his characters' situation. In other words it is displaced onto style. But the conceit, found in his early work, of a radically transforming vitality, a humanity pregnant with possibility affecting the social world first at the level of metaphor and subsequently at the literal level of a phoenix-like rebirth of values, defers here to a much more spare vision. The prolixity of his earlier plays is displaced by a calcified language which is no longer able to bear the weight of the muscular energy of a Maggie the Cat or a Serafina, still less the crude force of a Stanley Kowalski. Now words are used precisely, even primly, and constantly threaten to snap under the pressure of a neurotic fear. As in the plays of Albee, Pinter and Beckett, movement is reduced to a minimum—physical stasis standing as an image of constraint, as a denial of clear causality and as an assertion that the real drama operates in the mind (which reinvents the past, translates experience into meaning and imposes its own grid on experience, denying death and acting out its own necessary myth of immortality). His own penchant for symbolism is both exploited and mocked as the stage is dominated by a huge symbolic form, a monolithic figure that resists the actors' desire to dispense with it. The incompletions of the set underline the deconstructive thrust of the play which is a drama of entropy in which character, plot and language slowly disintegrate.

The play establishes several levels of "reality." Not only is there a play-within-the-play, with its supposed but invisible audience, but there is another posited audience addressed by one of the characters: "Of course," observes Felice, in an opening speech, "you realize that I'm trying to catch you and hold you with an opening monologue that has to be extended through several—rather arbitrary—transitions." The attenuations of the real become not only a strategy of the play but a basic assumption working to give a translucence to character and a neurotic hesitancy to action. For the Williams of *The Glass Menagerie* and *Streetcar* a substantial reality was needed, a hard-edged and threatening world just beyond the frame of the action, pressing hard upon character until it was forced to render up its essential meaning in the battle to sustain itself. Now that sustaining crust has dissolved. The menace is no longer external. The model of a threatening reality and a desperate world of fiction no longer holds. The menace is equally within. The real is completely problematic. The tension dissipates and with it character.

The play takes place in "an unspecified locality"—that well known pull-in for so many playwrights of the 1970s. The characters are never seen outside the context of the theatre. Felice addresses the audience directly, asking it to "Imagine the curtain is down." The audience is, therefore, invited to collaborate in the process of invention, and therefore, of course, to theatricalise itself. Instead of accepting fiction as reality it is asked to accept reality as a fiction. The curtain, the interface of fiction and reality, becomes itself a fiction. The two worlds can no longer be kept apart.

The boundary remains the area which fascinates Williams but now it expands to become a total world. There are no longer any clearly definable worlds to be kept apart. Even the characters' names—Clare and Felice—support a sexual ambiguity which is rooted in more than Williams's own sensibility. The androgynous is itself an embodiment of the erosion of definition. Clare remembers little of their past except a series of frontiers on their journey from one now-forgotten place to their present indefinite situation. There is a certain desperation behind the play. In the person of an "old, old painter . . . seated in *rigor mortis* before a totally blank canvas, tea kettle boiled dry," he creates a figure who represents his own self-doubts but also his fear that art itself is in a state of collapse. The blank canvas stands less for pregnant possibility than a kind of stunned silence. The idea of framed experience, of order, no matter how arbitrary, can no longer be sustained. In any one moment it may be possible to suspend time but only at the cost of suspending life. And so the ironically named Felice and Clare, like Vladimir and Estragon in *Waiting for Godot*, pass the time performing familiar rituals to keep the idea of chaos at bay. Improvisation may be the sign of vitality but it is equally a threat of dissolution, and Clare is as frightened of a disruption of the pattern as Faulkner's Bengy had been in the *The Sound and the Fury*. And so she fears the "chaos of improvisation, new speeches thrown at me like stones, as if I'd been condemned to be stoned to death."

The central conceit is clearly the familiar one that life is itself a performance that we are condemned to enact. We are fated to play ourselves as Clare is told she must "play" Clare. "Our performance," Felice acknowledges, "must continue. No escape." They thus play out their lives on a stage dominated by the vast dumb presence of a giant statue—a huge immovable construction with neither function nor life but whose existence creates an irony simply through the disproportion of size. As a metaphysical parable the play rests on a cliché. The literalness with which the metaphor is enacted suggests a potentially disabling banality. It is redeemed by the fact that it incorporates its own critique. The neat rationalism of metaphor is itself a victim of a world reduced to fictionality and even the allegorical pattern disassembles itself in such a wholly relativistic world. Felice remarks, as many of Williams's protagonists might have done, "I don't do lunatic things. I have to pretend there's some sanity here," but in the context of the play even this can be taken as primary evidence of insanity. Both Clare and Felice fear confinement and yet in a mental hospital the latter had experienced "the comforts, the security, the humanizing influence" of what Clare calls "locked doors." This is the familiar Williams paradox. Confinement and insanity have their advantages. They relieve one of the terrors that come from venturing beyond the known, from crossing frontiers. But they do so through an induced narcosis. What is sacrificed is "being aware of what's going on in our lives." However, in the context of this play that awareness is denied by the very terms of the characters' existence.

The Two Character Play becomes not merely the title of the play-within-the-play but an accurate description of the play that is their lives. Its lack of an ending is thus a natural consequence of their own desperately sustained existence. The characters rebel against "this metaphor that you are trying to catch me in, but I refuse to be caught!" But there is, of course, no choice.

The echoes of the vault in which they are supposedly trapped are equally those of a reflexive art and a reflexive life. There is no external world. Art and life are part of a continuum. The elegiac note which Clare detects applies to art and life equally. Her announcement that "I am going to find the way out" is merely ironic since the only escape lies through a bullet from the gun incorporated into the play at the level of plot and symbol. The darkness beyond the dimly lit stage is the only way out, and the terror of that is greater than that of the stage itself. The theatre is a prison but so, too, is the life which it supposedly reflects but for which it is in effect a paradigm. The anguished cry with which Clare responds to her situation is the prototypical sound of her humanity but it is also the essence of Williams's theatre as he sees it. In a comment quoted on the dust-jacket, Williams has said, "I think [it] is my most beautiful play since *Streetcar*, and I've never stopped working on it. I think it is a major work . . . it is a *cri de coeur*, but then all creative work, all life, in a sense, is a *cri de coeur*." The play ends with the brother and sister desperately trying to sustain their invented world as the lights fade—a fading of which they are fully conscious. "Magic is the habit of our existence," they announce together as they accept the fading of the lights "as a death, somehow transcended." The final remark is an apt description of Williams's own conviction. It is, moreover, an assertion of faith which distinguishes his characters, finally, from those of Beckett and Pinter. They are granted, if not full knowledge, then at least full self-awareness. They recognise the ironies that constitute their world and live them out. The phoenix is no longer an appropriate image, but perhaps Sisyphus would be. No longer do his characters "rage against the dying of the light." They accept their situation, but part of the burden laid upon them is the unavoidable desire to transform their world, to impose pattern on chaos. And this, after all, is the essence equally of the absurd, the Sisyphean victory.

Writing in 1959 Williams confessed that for him writing itself had always been "an escape from a world of reality in which I felt acutely uncomfortable." Like his characters he retreated into imagination which became "my cave, my refuge." By the time of *Out Cry* such a clear distinction between the real and the imagined no longer held. The entire set is now dramatised as simultaneously protective cave and prison. The imagination no longer presses back against a palpable reality. The mind generates its own environment. This is, if you like, a conversation between the male and female sides of Williams's sensibility. They conjoin in a neurotic fear. This is the world of Blanche DuBois after she has left the Kowalski household on the arm of the gentleman doctor and entered the mental hospital, which then becomes the setting for her theatricalising imagination.

Tennessee Williams's characters have always trodden the dangerous border between the real and the imagined, and the peculiar force of his work derives precisely from the doomed act of will with which his protagonists resist the fact of defeat or, occasionally and less believably, force a victory of sorts, a desperate compromise with time. The power of sexuality, at times therapeutic and redemptive, at times an image of determinism, gives his work its particular excitement. In his best work his over-poetic language and naive use of symbolism are kept in check by an imagination which if melodramatic is also capable of fine control. The collapse of that control, the growth of a self-pity which placed his own plight too nakedly at the centre of attention, the distintegration of his personality, eventually destroyed the honesty and perspective that enabled him to make Stanley Kowalski a worthy adversary for Blanche DuBois in *Streetcar*, and Laura's mother a compassionate friend as well as a shrill accuser of her daughter in *The Glass Menagerie*.

The confidence with which he started his career had long since drained away. In an essay in 1978 he wrote that he was convinced that no artist could "in the least divert" government "from a fixed course toward the slagheap remnants of once towering cities." He identified an "unconscious death-wish" on the part of those in power which the artist was powerless to resist, and indeed chose to trace this back to a specific historical moment: "civilization, at least as a long-term prospect, ceased to exist with the first nuclear blast at Hiroshima and Nagasaki." Seen thus his work becomes an account of the struggle for survival of those who find themselves living after the collapse of civilisation. But where once some temporary truce seemed possible, at this point personal crises and national decline seemed to promise nothing but extinction. He continued to assert the significance of the artist, insisting that "I presume to insist that there must be somewhere truth to be pursued each day with words that are misunderstood and feared because they are the words of an Artist, which must always remain a word most compatible with the word Revolutionary, and so be more than a word," but the conviction had gone. "Graceful defeat" remained his objective but grace is itself a primary victim of the world which he chose to describe throughout much of the 1970s.

Then, like Arthur Miller, whose *The American Clock* was set in the 1930s that had moulded his imaginative world, Tennessee Williams returned, in the late 1970s, to the decade in which his talent had also been forged. *Vieux Carré* (1977) was set in the winter of 1938 and the spring of 1939, *A Lovely Sunday for Creve Coeur* (1979) in the St Louis of his youth and *Something Cloudy, Something Clear* (1981) in the summer of 1940.

Vieux Carré is a recreation of Williams's own time spent in New Orleans. Set in a rooming house (as *The Glass Menagerie* was to have been), it offers a portrait of a collection of misfits, killing their loneliness as best they can, a loneliness "inborn and inbred to the bone." Nightingale is a homosexual painter dying of tuberculosis; Jane, a woman desperate for affection and dying of what seems to be leukemia; Mrs Wire, a "solitary old woman cared for by no one"; Sky, a young man as in love with long distance as Mrs Wingfield's husband had been in *The Glass Menagerie*. And at the centre is the Writer, discovering a homosexual identity and displaying his literary talent as one means to neutralise the "affliction" of loneliness. Mrs Wire's comment that "there's so much loneliness in this house that you can hear it" is, indeed, an understatement, for the play presses a familiar Williams theme to the point of parody. It offers a self-portrait which, for all its recognition of a degree of cruelty in the human make-up (his observation that "A man has got to face everything some time and call it by its true name" is a piece of gratuitous cruelty that the play rejects), is sentimental to a degree.

A Lovely Sunday for Creve Coeur concerns yet further lonely and desperate people whose fate, in the words of one of the characters from *Vieux Carré*, is to "offer himself and not be accepted, not by anyone ever!" As in so much else of Williams's work his own concerns are expressed through the sensibility of a woman. Like so much else of his work it is concerned with the compromises forced on the individual by a life which refuses to satisfy a desperate longing for human contact, or to fulfil the aspirations of those who long for a dream but exist in a harsh reality.

In *Something Cloudy, Something Clear* Williams returned to the summer of 1940 but in a sense it was a play which also looked forward to death. Set in Provincetown, it concerns August, a young writer who lives in a shack on the dunes, and who writes his first play while simultaneously making a bid for the attentions of a male dancer called Kip. But the latter is dying of a brain tumour while his friend and protector Clare is suffering from diabetes. Death is in the air and when Clare asks August how long he will continue to work he replies that he will go on until he dies of exhaustion. And so the beginning and end of Williams's career curve towards one another, the beginning implying the end, death still being resisted by desire, though now that desire is seen more clearly as the writer's passion for creation. But, then, sex and writing had always been equally potent images for one another in his work; the momentary completions, the satisfaction achieved only to be dissipated, always constituted appropriate symbols of the imperfect satisfactions of human relationships and the artistic experience alike. And yet, by the same token, these moments of consonance remained the only justification for life's continuance, for the endless struggle with determinism which seemed to him otherwise to define the nature of daily life.

As he grew older so he seemed to have been increasingly haunted by the past. His thematic concern with lost youth, loneliness, a failing public appeal and the collapse of those fictions with which people seek to neutralise an insistent reality acquired a personal relevance more acute than earlier in his career. The romantic concern with fading beauty, illness, the writer whose work is created at the cost of personal survival—always there in his work—began to seem a patent sentimentality. It smacked of self-pity. The decadence which he described and celebrated is that of the artist finding truth in appearance and even humiliation, but it is equally that of a writer whose personal neuroses invaded his work too completely.

There is a persuasive truth to the comments of his one-time collaborator and lover Donald Windham who, in 1977, wrote that:

> Hardly anyone succeeds as an artist in America without first devoting his whole being to the problems of obscurity and failure. Tennessee did this for ten years before 1945; then the tables were turned and overnight he was faced with a whole new set of problems. He controlled them remarkably well for the next five years. But a great deal of his strength must have gone into battles other than those of creation. When his emotional material began to run low, the priceless "by-product of existence" to be in need of replenishing, and he was forced to come out of his shell of unawareness, he found himself, both by design and fate, in a totally different world from that which had enclosed him and nourished his heart before . . . by 1955 I believe that both he and his work were suffering from the manoeuvers he was making to protect himself and it.

The early work came directly out of the tensions in his own experience. It was in a sense the public dimension of a series of private conflicts. Blanche's neurotic drive, her fear of mortality, her destructive grip on a life charged with significance by a brittle sexuality were Williams's own; but then so, too, was the implacable logic which led him to relinquish her to insanity and stasis. A cavalier sensibility and a puritan spirit coexist and the result is an oddly Manichean view of human affairs which frequently finds its correlative in terms of the *mise-en-scène*. In the persons of Laura, Blanche and Alma (in *The Glass Menagerie*, *Streetcar*, and *Summer and Smoke*) he confesses to his own sense of historicity while in the very process, as a playwright, of staking his claim to contemporary attention. For a few years, perhaps a decade, these tensions seem to have addressed a similar ambivalence in the American sensibility. Certainly the political persecutions of the 1950s were in part a debate about national identity (the Un-American Activities Com-

mittee placing the definition of Americanness on the agenda) as they were
equally an attempt to accommodate older models of private and public be-
haviour to the new realities of post-war existence. It was a society on the
brink of change, uncertain as to direction and purpose. National myths were
up for debate. The right of dissent—the legitimacy of marching to a different
drummer—was challenged by those who regarded political and social cohe-
sion as a virtue. And when Laura's unicorn lost its horn—stamped on by a
young man on the make—it stood as an appropriate image of that new
conformity which equally alarmed Arthur Miller. There is no place for
Blanche in the pragmatics of the new world, except as sexual commodity.
And, for many, exchange values were precisely in process of replacing human
values. However, as in *Summer and Smoke*, Williams acknowledged the need
to adapt. He saw the risk in his own spiritual absolutism. So, too, did Miller
and many of those who fought against a new moral conformity while fully
aware of the danger of their own idealism. Thus, I suggest that for a few
brief years not merely did Williams's own private debates generate a drama
luminous with his own psychic, sexual, social and spiritual contradictions
but he also touched a nerve in the national sensibility in a way that only
Miller otherwise succeeded in doing. Williams has confessed to feeling a
deep chasm between himself and all other people, even deeper than the
relatively ordinary ones of homosexuality and being an artist, but that condition of "alienation" was scarcely unfamiliar in a culture in which the word
was used with some abandon in the 1950s and 1960s.

In the following decades, however, his concerns seemed to exist to one
side of those that commanded public attention. The urgencies of Vietnam
seem to have passed him by, except for a growing apocalypticism. The special
world which he wrote about now tended to seem irrelevant rather than
compellingly linked to national trauma. And yet the signs of recovery were
there. *Out Cry* responded to a shift in artistic concern equally apparent in
the novel, while the return, in his final plays, to the experiences of his youth
suggested a desire to recover the lost power and ambiguous tensions of his
early career. It was just such a tactic which had unlocked O'Neill's artistic
powers. Not the least of the ironies of his death was that it denied us the
opportunity of seeing Williams wrestle with his own demons, though a late
play—*Clothes for a Summer Hotel* (1980)—and a last screenplay—*Secret Places
of the Heart*—suggest the possible direction of a career peremptorily ended
by an ironic accident.

There is something rather more inevitable than ironic in the fact that
Williams should turn, at the end of his career, to Scott Fitzgerald and Zelda
for the subject of his play *Clothes for a Summer Hotel*. Their lives were too

close, in some respects, to his own for the parallels not to be examined. In part it was a matter of the all too obvious proximity of insanity as an immediate fact and potential fate; in part it was a recognition of their shared perception of life as a losing game and art as a structure of meaning placed under constant threat.

Clothes for a Summer Hotel is set in the Highland Hospital, the asylum in which Zelda lived, and, finally, died, in a fire which swept the building in 1947. The image of a retreat which finally becomes destructive was a familiar one in Williams's work and, as *Out Cry* had implied, the origin of a self-doubt which now applied directly to his work. And this play, like *Out Cry*, places the processes of the theatre in the foreground. Thus, at the beginning of the play, one of Fitzgerald's friends—Gerald Murphy—announces its running time while Zelda's desperate fictions, which both sustain and destroy, are finally not so easily separable from the illusions of the writer who, we are pointedly told, "creates" her. So she has to "play" her meeting with Scott—drawn to the asylum by erroneous accounts of her recovery— as Clare and Felice had acted out their own dramas. And she accuses him of being a predator, appropriating her life for his fiction, as Mrs Venable had required the sacrifice of Catharine, in *Suddenly Last Summer*, and as Williams accused himself of the appropriation of Rose's life for his own art. Yet, for all this, the play equally stands as a justification of fiction, though now as an agent of truth and no longer simply as a tactic of survival. As the young Intern, who at times is also an incarnation of Zelda's French lover, remarks, "Shadows of lives, tricks of light, sometimes illuminate things." This same point is, in effect, underscored by an Author's Note, ostensibly indicating the nature of Zelda's attempts to establish contact but equally a justification of his own artistic life and of the indirections but also the performatic integrity of theatre itself:

> Zelda must somehow suggest the desperate longing of the "insane" to communicate something of the private world to those from whom they're secluded. The words are mostly blown away by the wind . . . but the eyes—imploring though proud—the gestures, trembling though rigid with the urgency of their huge need, must win the audience to her inescapably . . . the present words given her are tentative: they may or may not suffice in themselves: the presentation—performance—must.

And yet the roles in which Williams, no less than Scott and Zelda, allowed himself to be trapped constituted an ironic distortion of this desire to communicate through the masks of performance. Thus Blanche's Belle Reve becomes the Reve Bleu of this play, the scene of Zelda's adultery, an image of betrayal rather than truth; her lover is an aviator, flight being as much his image of freedom as it was Williams's. But for him, too, that flight is a denial of some necessary contact.

Zelda is aware of the extent to which identity itself is a careful construct, a fiction elaborated partly by others and partly by social necessity. As she observes, "I know that I must resume the part created for me. Mrs F. Scott Fitzgerald." But, she asks, "If he makes of me a monument with his carefully arranged words, is that my life?" And yet for a writer that is essentially the dilemma—to create a factitious world which is not sealed against experience—just as in another sense it is the paradox of experience—to create a life which is not itself simply a pastiche of conventions, role-playing and self-deceit. As Zelda complains, "All photographs are a poor likeness," lacking the glow of memory. But memory is no closer to that reality, which now begins to seem an inadequate stimulus for the imagined self, which is in effect fictionalised, reconstructed, in the very process of perception. And so the stage set itself dissolves, reforms and fragments. Memory fades by turn into insanity, into realistic dialogue and into a self-conscious acknowledgement of a governing fictionality. If Zelda's (and Williams's) "huge, cloudy symbols of a high romance" are placed under pressure, then so, too, are the supposed solidities they are taken to represent. And the erosion of that boundary threatens a final collapse into insanity or a denial of the distinction which that word implies.

Nonetheless, a modernist conviction remains, not merely as to the imagination's power to resist the real but as to its ability to vindicate an existence whose coherences are themselves ultimately threatening. Thus, Zelda suggests that "Between the first wail of an infant and the last gasp of the dying— it's all an arranged pattern of submission to what's been prescribed for us unless we escape into madness or into acts of creation." But invention and madness are intimately related. For if "Romantics" will not settle for "acceptance," then "Liquor, madness [are]more or less the same thing," and then "We're abandoned or we're put away, and if put away, why, then, fantasy runs riot." And this is precisely the danger of the vertiginous path that Williams walked, for on the one hand was the pure anarchy of fantasy and on the other "what's called real—a rock! Cold, barren. To be endured only briefly." The challenge is to sustain a "vision" which will neither be betrayed into uncontrolled images nor earthed by a prosaic reality. And yet fictions also have their coercions. As Zelda cries out at the end of the play, addressing her husband, himself aware of his own fragile grasp on experience: "I'm not your book! Anymore! *I can't be your book anymore!*" Her only release from other people's fictions, however, lies through her own death, and, writing in 1980, just three years before his death, Williams recognised that a similar paradox applied to his own life.

There is a subtlety to *Clothes for a Summer Hotel* missing from so much of the work which he produced in the 1960s and 1970s. The elegiac tone seems to suggest the degree to which he was now able to recognise and to some extent reconcile the tensions and even contradictions in his own art and life. And the result seems to be a recovery of something of the simplicity and power of his early work as he reached back not only into the past but into the origin of his own artistic concerns.

One of Williams's last works, *Secret Places of the Heart*, a screenplay set, for the most part, in a mental hospital, seems an attempt to lay some familiar ghosts to rest. It has an elegiac tone. In a sense it brings us full circle, back to the world of *The Glass Menagerie*. It is as though we followed Laura, after the candles of her life had been snuffed out. And if that play had been a displaced account of her sister's life it is hard not to see *Secret Places of the Heart* as an attempt both to acknowledge his own ambiguous feelings towards Rose, sequestered for more than forty years, and also to confront in himself elements of that hysteria and fear which had closed the door so implacably on her life.

Janet, former wife of Olaf Svenson, lives in St Carmine's Sanatorium, a private mental hospital run by Catholic nuns. She lives a partially narcotised existence, but there is a tenuous and fragile sense of solidarity between those who find themselves so stranded. The high point of her life is provided by her husband's visits. But he, himself, is a highly nervous man and finds the hospital frightening. It is too close to his own neurotic fears of constriction to be borne with any equanimity. He lives with another woman, Alicia, who constantly urges him to break away from his wife. The film is concerned with Olav's attempt to tell Janet that he is to move away from the area, that she will be receiving no more visits. He takes her for one last trip beyond the walls of the institution, but it is disastrous, turning her catatonic and him almost speechless.

Indeed language becomes a central theme of the play as Janet had been a speech therapist whose skills and love had given Sven access to words. It is impossible not to see the filmscript as, in some sense at least, Williams's acknowledgement of a debt to Rose. Just as in *The Glass Menagerie* he had made a connection between Tom's freedom as a writer and his sister's entombment in the St. Louis apartment so now Sven's articulateness is presented as a gift of the woman trapped in the St. Louis sanatorium. In both cases the two are connected by an odd blend of guilt and love, and it is hard not to feel Williams's own ambiguous response to Rose and in particular the link between her silence (social and at times literal) and his own public articulateness. The sense of panic which overcomes Sven seems very close to that which Williams himself confessed to feeling on occasion, just as Janet's fear of death mirrors his own. The filmscript does not, however, end in total despair, though her world does seem to have been effectively destroyed. Her gentleman caller will not come again but there is a level on which some final adjustment has been made which does not represent mere capitulation. At first when she returns from her disastrous trip she sits in the rocking chair which has been established earlier as a symbol of the slowing rhythms of life, a fast approaching death. She sits silent and defeated. But in the final moments of the screenplay she rises from the chair, clutching a bunch of roses (whose association with his sister's name made them an image of life throughout his work), and joins the other inmates. The final word is given to her. It is an affirmation. In reply to one of the patients who welcomes her "hooome!" she replies, as a note indicates, resolutely, "Yes." At the end of his life it was an acceptance of the limits of freedom, of the fact of death and of the necessity to live on the far side of despair. It was a gesture of reconciliation with what life had done to Rose and to himself. Like the name of a compassionate nurse in this final refuge, it is an act of "Grace," and a fitting elegy for his life and his art. And if his characters are in some way at their most sincere and honest when their language fails them, this seems to emerge from a conviction, equally embraced by Harold Pinter, that the more acute an experience the less articulate its expression. And if this has clear implications for the writer for whom words are a necessary but fragile instrument, he had shown his awareness of this as early as *The Glass Menagerie*—as he had throughout a career in which the dramatic image was made to play a central and liberating role.

Jean Genet advocated the siting of theatres next to cemeteries. As an image this precisely captures Williams's sense both of the fact which gives birth to the self-dramatising sensibility of the individual and the public theatrical act. It is the fact of death and, even more, the neurotic fear of death, that provokes the theatrical impulse. It is not merely that vitality, the public discharge of energy, the reshaping of anarchic tendencies into satisfactory form, are counterposed to the deconstructive reality of death but that the invented self hopes to deceive death, hopes, by disguises, to evade the relentless drive of process, as the characters in *Camino Real* try to hide from the streetcleaners who are the agents of death. For Genet, pluralising himself, "We will have nothing to do with politics, entertainment, morality, etc.," and if, "in spite of ourselves, they step into the theatrical act, let them be driven out until all trace of them is gone." Williams was less rigorous. He was concerned with morality, though not with moralism, but that morality is generated by a respect for human need. It is a product of the void and a response to it. It becomes necessary not to compound the fact of that void. So that Williams was no antinomian. But unlike Miller he could imagine no abstraction to which the individual owes allegiance. Society represents only a threat, a compounding of absurdity. The only morality which he would sanction was that deriving from personal relationships. The sensibility is neurotically responsive because it must detect that human need. That the same sensitivity makes the self more vulnerable to social pressure and more acutely aware of its ultimate fate is the source of the romantic irony which pervades his work. There is, indeed, more than a little of Poe in Williams. Both men were obsessed with death to the extent that their own work was a self-conscious attempt to deny its authority and madness was an image of the delicate membrane which each believed separated the individual from knowledge of his or her own mortality.

For Genet the theatre is built on a paradox. It derives from awareness of a fact which should destroy its own premise: "If its origin is some dazzling moment in the author's experience, it is up to him to seize the lightning and, beginning with the moment of illumination, which reveals the void, to arrange a verbal architecture—that is, grammatical and ceremonial—slyly suggesting that from this void some semblance is snatched which reveals the void. It is from this paradox that Beckett's plays derive and to some extent Williams's also, though in most of his work he chose to resolve the paradox by asserting that the imagination, operating either through its powers of self-invention or through its sympathetic understanding of the solitariness of the other, is able to create a morality which is no less real for existing outside of time. But in *Out Cry* the implacable nature of the metaphor stands exposed. The plot of life is stifled, character is dislocated and disassembled, language hollowed out. The role-playing of art and life is presented as synonymous while logical developments of theatre, from simile to metonymy to metaphor (from as if, to a slice of life, to an enactment of life), which perhaps mimics the development of the individual, moves Williams to identify a level on which art and life not merely contain their own denial but are the primary source of their own absurdity. It is not merely, as Val Xavier in *Orpheus Descending* observes, that "We are all of us sentenced to imprisonment inside our own skins for life," but that the imagination, which is our primary bid for transcendence, is the essence of our self-torturing yearning for order and meaning. Clare and Felice perform themselves from a stage whose props contain no clue to their meaning in front of an empty auditorium. But, lacking anything else, they continue, falteringly, to repeat half-forgotten lines until the lights fade. Though he wrote subsequent plays, *Out Cry* is his valediction for the theatre not simply in the literal sense in which he lost his audience while being tied nonetheless to a craft, the significance of which he had come profoundly to doubt, but to the degree that he saw his own entrapment in the endless desire to create form from the formless. Earlier he had suggested that "the great and only possible dignity of a man lies in his power deliberately to choose certain moral values by which to live as steadfastly as if he, too, like a character in a play, were immured against the corrupting rush of time." He spoke of "the incontinent blaze of live theatre" as a celebration of a surviving, even triumphant human spirit. But he ended his career in self-doubt, as his own fictions seemed all too directly expressive of the degenerate and self-mocking fictions of the world which he had once imagined himself to be able to transcend through the simple but transforming mechanism of the imagination.

There is a terrible, empty gregariousness about his characters. They cling to one another with a desperation which is half touching and half pathetic, the more so since they are indeed one another's hell. Cooped up, in a bid for the therapy of relationship, they are terrified by a persistent claustrophobia. Like their author they seek the comfort of strangers but those strangers merely serve to remind them of a world of causality, of competing demands and remorseless process. They detect the signs of mortality. Faces are lined, eyes are surrounded by crow's feet. They fear the light. And yet the intimacy they seek in order to neutralise their loneliness inevitably results in exposure. The real intrudes, implacable, irresistible. The glass horn snaps, the paper lantern is torn from the lamp, the instinctive and necessary lie is revealed for what it is. There is only one possible direction left for them— a journey into pure imagination and madness, an apocalyptic flame in which the self is extinguished by embracing its own image. It is a familiar romantic stance: the self is annihilated by expanding to fill the available psychic and moral space. Sometimes the apocalypse is literal, a public role performed by the cruel and selfish whose pragmatics can find no room for the deviant; sometimes it is embraced as though there were some grace to be claimed by wilfully compounding the reductivism of positivist society and biological process alike. Williams's characters go to their martyrdom in play after play, tortured and crucified for their visions which are mistaken for lies. Desperately sexual beings, the consummation which they seek is nonetheless spiritual. The body they embrace is physical enough but what they seek is seldom simply sexual satisfaction. They long for completion. They seek to close the wound opened up by their birth. They try to cheat death but more often than not find themselves holding it to them. The compassion which they seek or dispense is not merely momentary; it snares them in time, inhibits that flight, that animal-like urge to escape, which is their own basic instinct.

In his early years as he travelled around the country struggling to make enough money to finance his writing, Williams carried with him *The Collected Poems of Hart Crane*. He must have found much which appealed to his own sensibility. In particular he must have recognised something of himself in Waldo Frank's description of the poet which appeared in the 1933 edition. For to him Crane "began naked and brave, in a cultural chaos, the subject of inchoate forces through which he rose to utterance. Cities, machines, the warring hungers of lonely and herded men, the passions released from defeated loyalties, were ever near to overwhelm the poet." His task, as Frank saw it, was "to bear and finally transfigure the world's impinging chaos." Williams saw his plight as essentially the same. Though temperamentally drawn to the defeated, he was, through the very process of writing, celebrating other values. Like Maggie in *Cat on a Hot Tin Roof* he was implicitly asserting that "my hat is still in the ring . . . What is the victory of a cat on a hot tin roof?—I wish I knew . . . Just staying on it, I guess, as long as she can." In play after play he dramatised his conviction that, in Maggie's words, "life has got to be allowed to continue even after the *dream* of life is—all over." Indeed that was his essential subject—life as a kind of rearguard action. He opted for neither truth nor illusion but for the need to resist. Maggie the cat uses truth; Blanche illusions. The writer meanwhile asserted the central importance of truths (Williams said that he found it painful and almost impossible to engage even in the ritual lies of personal politeness), but did so in plays which were themselves lies, factitious paradigms of social contact, illusions of order and purpose. He continued to rely on the kindness of strangers with whom he felt a momentary contact through the processes of art, but knew all too well the fragile and contingent nature of such relationships. For him, as for the characters of *Out Cry*, the stage was a world which appeared to offer a structure of meaning whose absence otherwise is the origin of personal neurosis and even hysteria. And if his confidence in that world was gradually eroded, not merely with the public decline of interest in his work but also with his own increasing sense of its arbitrary gestures and incomplete language, he was left with nowhere else to turn. Increasingly his plays became comments on one another. His characters, his language, his plots seemed to be rooted less in an experience external to the theatre than in his own earlier work. If he revisited his past it tended to be through texts, figures and images which were already transpositions of that past. Parody, pastiche and irony became his primary mode.

Like the two characters in *Out Cry* he seemed to be trapped in the theatre, endlessly recreating texts rather than reaching out into an experience external to art. Blanche DuBois increasingly seemed an apt expression of Williams's own sensibility, the neurotic intensity of his inventions, the desperate fascination with transforming the past, the need to act out a public myth of sensitivity assailed by a crude materialism if not an incipient barbarism, being evident in his life and art. His *Memoirs*, indeed, with their accounts of desperate sexuality, of drink and drugs, of the artist confronted with the inevitable compromises which transfigured his dreams, constituted simply another Williams drama, a play in which the central character transforms his life into art as a means of forcing it to render up some meaning beyond mere contingency. The *Memoirs*, like his plays, offered an opportunity to move to centre stage a man whose greatest fear was that he, and the world which he valued, had long since been relegated to the past, declared irrelevant by a society disinclined to value the poet, the homosexual or the dreamer except as licensed clown.

Writing in 1955, Williams had said:

> I think my work is good in exact relation to the degree of emotional tension which is released in it. In a sense, writing of this kind (lyric?) is a losing game, for steadily life takes away from you, bit by bit, step by step, the quality of fresh involvement, new, startling reactions to experience, the emotional reservoir is only rarely replenished by some crisis . . . and most of the time you arc just "paying out," draining off. To offset this, to some degree, usually not enough, is the accumulation of insight and "sophistication." Sometimes the heart dies deliberately, to avoid further pain.

Five years later he observed that "when the work of any kind of creative worker becomes tyrannically obsessive to the point of overshadowing his life, almost taking the place of it, he is in a hazardous situation. His situation is hazardous for the simple reason that the source, the fountainhead of his work, can only be his life." This risk proved real enough in Williams's own case. The gap between his art and his life, always small, narrowed still further. For when he entered his own play, as he did by appearing in *Small Craft Warnings*, he passed through a mirror and annihilated a crucial distinction. But he had always tended to dramatise his life. Indeed he made plans to dramatise his death. A codicil to his will reportedly provided for the disposition of his body as follows: it was to be "Sewn up in a clean white sack and dropped over board, twelve hours north of Havana, so that my bones may rest no too far from those of Hart Crane." But then perhaps his

heart had already died back there in the mid 1950s "to avoid further pain."
In the event this injunction seems to have been dropped from his will. What
did appear, apart from the seeds of future litigation, was a further reminder
of his attachment to his sister for part of his estate was to go towards her
maintenance and her "customary pleasures," including her shopping trips to
New York City.

In his *Memoirs* Williams asked himself, "What is it like being a writer?"
His reply was that "it is like being free . . . To be free is to have achieved
your life . . . it means to be a voyager here and there . . . It means the
freedom of being . . . Most of you belong to something that offers a stabilizing
influence: a family unit, a defined social position, employment in an organization, a more secure habit of existence." But, fearing constriction above
all else, Williams preferred to "live like a gypsy. I am a fugitive," he insisted.
"No place seems tenable to me for long anymore, not even my own skin."
In the end he could run no further and the personal relations on which he
relied had in large part failed him. At any rate he died alone in a hotel room,
a fugitive run to earth, a voyager who had found the only kind of freedom
he was ever likely to secure. The legless bird had finally touched the earth
and hence would never again soar above the "Terra Incognita."

In a poem published in his collection, *Androgyne, Mon Amour* (1977)
Williams defined his territory, his subject and his method:

> My mise-en-scene is the world
> within the world,
> the greenest of all green leaves
> at the center curled.
>
> I do not forbear to call
> on demons driven
> from mortal belief by the bells
> of a proper heaven.
>
> I ferret among the used
> and exhausted lot
> from the longing not wanted because
> it was haunted and hot.
>
> I want no purpose to own me
> but only to say
> I found these secretly burning
> along the way.

This girl who was lost but knew
more places than one.
this boy who was blind but grew
the interior sun.

Williams was that boy; his art the interior sun. And the girl? Who else but Rose and, beyond her, all those others working their way as best they can along the Camino Real.

Williams's reputation declined sharply in his later years. Undoubtedly this was in large part a fair reflection of the quality of his work which also suffered from his self-inflicted wounds. But it also said something about the culture in which he lived. Perhaps the most moving valedictory on Williams's work was that offered by one of America's best younger playwrights—David Mamet. As he observed, when Williams's "life and view of life became less immediately accessible, our gratitude was changed to distant reverence for a man whom we felt obliged—if we were to continue in our happy feelings toward him—to consider already dead." Perhaps this was inevitable but for Mamet there was a certain irony for Americans are, he observed, "a kind people living in a cruel country. We don't know how to show our love. [But] This was the subject of his plays, the greatest dramatic poetry in the American language. We thank him and we wish him, with love, the best we could have done and did not. We wish him what he wishes us: the peace that we are seeking." Despite the sentimentality which was a natural product of the occasion Mamet accurately identifies Williams's central theme and ultimate achievement.

Chronology

1911   Born Thomas Lanier Williams in Columbus, Mississippi.

1911–18   Lives with mother and sister Rose and maternal grandparents, as father is often away on business. They move often, finally settling in St. Louis, Missouri.

1927   Wins prize for essay, "Can a Good Wife Be a Good Sport?" then published in *Smart Set* magazine.

1928   Visits Europe with grandfather. First story published in *Weird Tales:* "The Vengeance of Nitocris."

1929   Enters University of Missouri. Wins honorable mention for first play, *Beauty Is the World.*

1931   Father withdraws him for flunking ROTC at university. Works at father's shoe company.

1935   Released from job after illness and recuperates at grandparents' house in Memphis, where his play *Cairo! Shanghai! Bombay!* is produced.

1936–37   Enters and is later dropped from Washington University, St. Louis. Enters University of Iowa. First full-length plays produced: *The Fugitive Kind* and *Candles to the Sun.* Prefrontal lobotomy performed on sister Rose.

1938   Graduates from University of Iowa.

1939   First uses name "Tennessee" on "The Field of Blue Children," published in *Story* magazine. Travels from New Orleans to California to Mexico to New Mexico to St. Louis. Awarded $1,000 Rockefeller grant. Begins new full-length play, *Battle of Angels.*

1940   Moves to New York to enroll in advanced playwrighting seminar taught by John Gassner at The New School.

1941–43 Takes various jobs in Provincetown, New York, Macon (Georgia), Jacksonville (Florida), and St. Louis. Begins *The Gentleman Caller* (later *The Glass Menagerie*.) Works at MGM as scriptwriter.

1944   Awarded $1,000 by the National Institute of Arts and Letters for *Battle of Angels*. *The Glass Menagerie* opens in Chicago on December 26.

1945   *The Glass Menagerie* opens in New York, wins New York Critics' Circle Award.

1946   *27 Wagons Full of Cotton and Other Plays* published.

1947   *A Streetcar Named Desire* opens in New York. *Summer and Smoke* opens in Dallas, Texas. Wins second New York Critics' Circle Award and Pulitzer Prize.

1948   *Summer and Smoke* opens in New York. *American Blues: Five Short Plays* published. *One Arm and Other Stories* published.

1950   *The Roman Spring of Mrs. Stone*, a novel, published. *The Rose Tattoo* opens in Chicago.

1951   *The Rose Tattoo* opens in New York, wins the Antoinette Perry (Tony) Award for best play. Film version of *A Streetcar Named Desire*, screenplay by Williams and Oscar Saul, released.

1953   *Camino Real* opens in New York.

1954   *Hard Candy: A Book of Stories* published.

1955   *Cat on a Hot Tin Roof* opens in New York. Wins third New York Critics' Circle Award and second Pulitzer Prize.

1956   *Baby Doll*, a film. *In the Winter of Cities*, poems, published. Father dies. Begins psychoanalysis.

1957   *Orpheus Descending* opens in New York.

1958   *Garden District (Something Unspoken* and *Suddenly Last Summer)* opens Off-Broadway. Film version of *Cat on a Hot Tin Roof* released.

1959   *Sweet Bird of Youth* opens in New York.

1960   *Period of Adjustment* opens in New York.

1961   *Night of the Iguana* opens in New York.

1962   Film version of *Sweet Bird of Youth* released. A one-act version of *The Milk Train Doesn't Stop Here Anymore* presented in Spoleto, Italy, at the Festival of Two Worlds.

1963   Full-length version of *Milk Train* opens in New York. Period of depression begins after death of his lover Frank Merlo.

1964   Film version of *The Night of the Iguana* released.

1966   *Slapstick Tragedy (The Mutilated* and *The Gnädiges Fraulein)* opens in New York.

1967   *The Two Character Play* opens in London. *The Knightly Quest: A Novella and Four Short Stories* published.

1968   *Kingdom of Earth (The Seven Descents of Myrtle)* opens in New York.

1969   *In the Bar of a Tokyo Hotel* opens Off-Broadway. Converts to Roman Catholicism. Stays three months in hospital in St. Louis after nervous collapse.

1970   *Dragon County: A Book of Plays* published.

1971   Revised version of *Two Character Play* called *Out Cry* opens in Chicago.

1972   *Small Craft Warnings* opens off-off-Broadway.

1973   *Out Cry* (a third revision of *Two Character Play*) opens in New York.

1974   *Eight Mortal Ladies Possessed: A Book of Stories* published.

1975   Receives the National Arts Club gold medal for literature. *Moise and the World of Reason*, a novel, is published. *The Red Devil Battery Sign* opens in Boston. Fourth version of *Two Character Play* opens Off-Off-Broadway. *Memoirs* published.

1976   Revised *Red Devil* opens in Vienna.

1977   *Vieux Carré* opens in New York.

1978   *Creve Coeur* opens in Charleston, South Carolina. *Where I Live: Selected Essays* published.

1979   *A Lovely Day for Creve Coeur*, revised version of *Creve Coeur*, opens in New York.

1980   *Clothes for a Summer Hotel* opens in Washington, D.C. Mother dies.

1981   *A House not Meant to Stand* opens in Chicago. *Something Cloudy Something Clear* opens in New York.

1982   Receives honorary degree from Harvard University.

1983   Dies in February.

Contributors

HAROLD BLOOM, Sterling Professor of the Humanities at Yale University, is the author of *The Anxiety of Influence, Poetry and Repression*, and many other volumes of literary criticism. His forthcoming study, *Freud: Transference and Authority*, attempts a full-scale reading of all of Freud's major writings. A MacArthur Prize Fellow, he is general editor of five series of literary criticism published by Chelsea House.

ALVIN B. KERNAN is A. W. Mellon Professor of Humanities at Princeton University. His books include critical studies of Shakespeare and of the genre of literary satire.

JOSEPH N. RIDDEL is Professor of English at the University of California at Los Angeles and the author of *The Clairvoyant Eye: The Poetry and Poetics of Wallace Stevens* and *The Inverted Bell: Modernism and the Counterpoetics of William Carlos Williams*.

ESTHER MERLE JACKSON is Professor of Theater and Drama at the University of Wisconsin at Madison. She is author of *The Broken World of Tennessee Williams* and studies of other American playwrights, including Maxwell Anderson and Amira Baraka (LeRoi Jones).

LEONARD QUIRINO is Professor of English at Western Connecticut State College, Danbury.

RUBY COHN is Professor of Comparative Drama at the University of California at Davis and the author of several book-length studies of Samuel Beckett.

ROBERT BECHTOLD HEILMAN is Professor Emeritus of English at the University of Washington in Seattle. He is the author of many studies on modern literature and on Shakespeare.

155

THOMAS L. KING is Professor of Communications Arts at James Madison University. He has been involved in several theatrical productions there and has appeared many times in productions of *The Glass Menagerie.*

JAMES COAKLEY is Associate Professor in the Department of Theater at Northwestern University.

ARTHUR GANZ is Associate Professor of English at the City College of New York and the author of *Realms of the Self.*

GILBERT DEBUSSCHER teaches English and American literature at the University of Brussels in Belgium. He is the author of *Edward Albee: Tradition and Renewal* and numerous articles on contemporary American theater.

C. W. E. BIGSBY is Reader in American Literature in the School of English and American Studies at the University of East Anglia in Norwich. His books include *Dada and Surrealism, Confrontation and Commitment: A Study of Contemporary American Drama, 1959–1966,* and *The Second Black Renaissance: Essays in Black Literature* as well as studies of Tom Stoppard, Joe Orton, and Edward Albee.

Bibliography

Atkinson, Brooks. "Theatre: Early Williams." *The New York Times*, November 22, 1956.

Bentley, Eric. *In Search of Theatre*. New York: Knopf, 1953.

———. *The Life of the Drama*. New York: Atheneum, 1964.

Brandt, George. "Cinematic Structure in the Works of Tennessee Williams." In *American Theatre*, edited by J. R. Brown and B. Harris, 163–88. London: Edward Arnold, 1967.

Brooks, Charles B. "The Comic Tennessee Williams." *The Quarterly Journal of Speech* 44 (October 1958): 275–81.

Brustein, Robert. *Seasons of Discontent; Dramatic Opinions, 1959–1965*. New York: Simon & Schuster, 1965.

———. "Why American Plays Are Not Literature." In *Writing in America*. New Brunswick, N.J.: Rutgers University Press, 1960.

Cohn, Ruby. *Dialogue in American Drama*. Bloomington: Indiana University Press, 1971.

Corrigan, Mary Ann. "Memory, Dream and Myth in the Plays of Tennessee Williams." *Renascence* 28 (Spring 1976): 155–67.

Debusscher, Gilbert. "Tennessee Williams's Unicorn Broken Again." *Revue belge de Philologie et d'Histoire* 49 (1971): 875–85.

———. *York Notes on Tennessee Williams:* The Glass Menagerie. London: Longman, York Press, 1982.

Dickenson, Hugh. "Tennessee Williams: Orpheus as Savior." In *Myth on the Modern Stage*, 278–309. Urbana: University of Illinois Press, 1969.

Donahue, Francis. *The Dramatic World of Tennessee Williams*. New York: Ungar, 1964.

Driver, Tom F. "Drama." *The Christian Century* 74, April 10, 1957, 455–56.

Durham, Frank. "Tennessee Williams: Theatre Poet in Prose." *South Atlantic Bulletin* 36 (March 1971): 3–16.

Falk, Signi Lenea. *Tennessee Williams*. New York: Twayne, 1961.

Fedder, Norman J. *The Influence of D. H. Lawrence on Tennessee Williams*. The Hague: Mouton, 1966.

Fritscher, John J. "Some Attitudes, and a Posture: Religious Metaphor and Ritual in Tennessee Williams's Query of the American God." *Modern Drama* 13 (September 1970): 201–15.

Ganz, Arthur. "The Desperate Morality of the Plays of Tennessee Williams." *American Scholar* 31 (Spring 1962): 278–94.

Gassner, John. *Directions in Modern Theatre and Drama.* New York: Holt, Rinehart & Winston, 1965.

———. *Theatre at the Crossroads.* New York: Holt, Rinehart & Winston, 1960.

Gilman, Richard. *Common and Uncommon Masks: Writings on Theatre 1962–1970.* New York: Random House, 1971.

Howell, Elmo. "The Function of Gentlemen Callers: A Note on Tennessee Williams's *The Glass Menagerie.*" *Notes on Mississippi Writers* 2 (Winter 1970): 83–90.

Hughes, Catharine R. *Tennessee Williams: A Biography.* Englewood Cliffs, N.J.: Prentice-Hall, 1978.

Hurley, Paul J. "Tennessee Williams: The Playwright as Social Critic." *The Theatre Annual* 21 (1964): 40–56.

Jackson, Esther Merle. *The Broken World of Tennessee Williams.* Madison: University of Wisconsin Press, 1965.

———. "The Problem of Form in the Drama of Tennessee Williams." *College Language Association Journal* 4, no. 1 (September 1960): 8–21.

Jones, Robert Emmet. "Tennessee Williams's Early Heroines." *Modern Drama* 2 (December 1959): 211–19.

Kazan, Elia. "Notebook for *A Streetcar Named Desire.*" In *Directors on Directing,* edited by Toby Cole and Helen Krich Chinoy. New York: Bobbs-Merrill, 1963.

Krutch, Joseph Wood. "Why the O'Neill Star Is Rising." *New York Times Magazine,* March 19, 1961.

Lumley, Frederick. *New Trends in 20th Century Drama: A Survey Since Ibsen and Shaw.* 3d ed. New York: Oxford University Press, 1967.

Miller, Arthur. "The Shadows of the Gods: A Critical View of the American Theatre." *Harper's* 217 (August 1958): 35–43. Reprinted in *American Playwrights on Drama,* edited by Horst Frenz. New York: Hill & Wang, 1965.

Miller, Jordan Y., ed. *Twentieth Century Interpretations of* A Streetcar Named Desire: *A Collection of Critical Essays.* Englewood Cliffs, N.J.: Prentice-Hall, 1971.

Napieralski, Edmund A. "Tennessee Williams's *The Glass Menagerie:* The Dramatic Metaphor." *Southern Quarterly* 16 (1977): 1–12.

Nelson, Benjamin. *Tennessee Williams: The Man and His Work.* New York: Obolensky, 1961.

Parker, R. B. *Twentieth Century Interpretations of* The Glass Menagerie: *A Collection of Critical Essays.* Englewood Cliffs, N.J.: Prentice-Hall, 1983.

Popkin, Henry. "The Plays of Tennessee Williams." *Tulane Drama Review* 4 (March 1960): 45–64.

———. "Tennessee Williams Reexamined." *Arts in Virginia* 11 (Spring 1971): 2–5.

Scott, Nathan A., Jr. *The Broken Center: Studies in the Theological Horizon of Modern Literature.* New Haven: Yale University Press, 1966.

Stanton, Stephen, ed. *Tennessee Williams: A Collection of Critical Essays.* Englewood Cliffs, N.J.: Prentice-Hall, 1977.

Starnes, Leland. "The Grotesque Children of *The Rose Tattoo.*" *Modern Drama* 12 (February 1970): 357–69.

Tharpe, Jac L., ed. *Tennessee Williams: A Tribute.* Jackson: University Press of Mississippi, 1977.

Tischler, Nancy M. *Tennessee Williams: Rebellious Puritan*. New York: Citadel Press, 1961.

Traubitz, Nancy B. "Myth as a Basis of Dramatic Structure." *Modern Drama* 19 (March 1976): 55–66.

Tynan, Kenneth. "American Blues: The Plays of Arthur Miller and Tennessee Williams." *Encounter* (England) 2 (May 1954): 13–19.

Vidal, Gore. "Selected Memories of the Glorious Bird and the Golden Age." *The New York Review of Books*, February 5, 1976, 13–18.

Vowles, Richard B. "Tennessee Williams and Strindberg." *Modern Drama* 1 (December 1958): 166–71.

———. "Tennessee Williams: The World of His Imagery." *Tulane Drama Review* 3 (December 1958): 51–56.

Weales, Gerard. *Tennessee Williams*. Minneapolis: University of Minnesota Press, 1965. rev. ed. 1974.

Weigand, Hermann J., ed. *Insight IV: Analyses of Modern British and American Drama*. Frankfurt: Hirchgraben, 1975.

Acknowledgments

"Truth and Dramatic Mode in *A Streetcar Named Desire*" (originally entitled "Truth and Dramatic Mode in the Modern Theater: Chekhov, Pirandello, and Williams") by Alvin B. Kernan from *Modern Drama* 1, no. 2 (September 1958), © 1958 by the University of Toronto, Graduate Centre for the Study of Drama. Reprinted by permission of *Modern Drama*.

"*A Streetcar Named Desire*—Nietzsche Descending" by Joseph N. Riddel from *Modern Drama* 5, no. 4 (February 1963), © 1963 by the University of Toronto, Graduate Centre for the Study of Drama. Reprinted by permission of *Modern Drama*.

"The Synthetic Myth" by Esther Merle Jackson from *The Broken World of Tennessee Williams* by Esther Merle Jackson, © 1965 by Esther Merle Jackson. Reprinted by permission of the University of Wisconsin Press.

"Tennessee Williams's Persistent *Battle of Angels*" by Leonard Quirino from *Modern Drama* 11, no. 1 (May 1968), © 1968 by the University of Toronto, Graduate Centre for the Study of Drama. Reprinted by permission of *Modern Drama*.

"The Garrulous Grotesques of Tennessee Williams" by Ruby Cohn from *Dialogue in American Drama* by Ruby Cohn, © 1971 by Indiana University Press. Reprinted by permission.

"The Middle Years" (originally entitled "Tennessee Williams [1914–]") by Robert Bechtold Heilman from *The Iceman, the Arsonist, and the Troubled Agent: Tragedy and Melodrama on the Modern Stage* by Robert Bechtold Heilman, © 1973 by the University of Washington Press. Reprinted by permission.

"Irony and Distance in *The Glass Menagerie*" by Thomas L. King from *Educational Theatre Journal* 25, no. 2 (May 1973), © 1973 by the American Theatre Association, Inc. Reprinted by permission of the Johns Hopkins University Press.

"Time and Tide on the *Camino Real*" by James Coakley from *Tennessee Williams: A Tribute*, edited by Jac Tharpe, © 1977 by the University Press of Mississippi. Reprinted by permission of the University Press of Mississippi.

"A Desperate Morality" (originally entitled "Williams and Miller") by Arthur Ganz from *Realms of the Self: Variations on a Theme in Modern Drama* by Arthur Ganz, © 1980 by New York University. Reprinted by permission of New York University Press.

161

" 'Minting Their Separate Wills': Tennessee Williams and Hart Crane" by Gilbert Debusscher from *Modern Drama* 26, no. 4 (December 1983), © 1983 by the University of Toronto, Graduate Centre for the Study of Drama. Reprinted by permission of *Modern Drama*.

"Valedictory" (originally entitled "Tennessee Williams") by C. W. E. Bigsby from *A Critical Introduction to Twentieth-Century American Drama 2: Tennessee Williams, Arthur Miller, Edward Albee* by C. W. E. Bigsby, © 1984 by C. W. E. Bigsby. Reprinted by permission of the author and Cambridge University Press.

Index